3-Fabric Quilts

❖ QUICK TECHNIQUES FOR ❖
SIMPLE PROJECTS

Leni Levenson Wiener

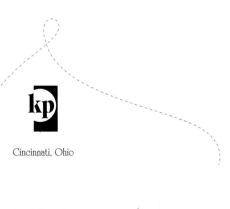

kp

Cincinnati, Ohio

www.fwmedia.com

15 14 13 12 11   5 4 3 2 1

DISTRIBUTED IN CANADA BY FRASER DIRECT
100 Armstrong Avenue
Georgetown, ON, Canada L7G 5S4
Tel: (905) 877-4411

DISTRIBUTED IN THE U.K. AND EUROPE BY F&W MEDIA INTERNATIONAL
Brunel House, Newton Abbot, Devon, TQ12 4PU, England
Tel: (+44) 1626 323200, Fax: (+44) 1626 323319
Email: enquiries@fwmedia.com

DISTRIBUTED IN AUSTRALIA BY CAPRICORN LINK
P.O. Box 704, S. Windsor NSW, 2756 Australia
Tel: (02) 4577-3555

ISBN-13: 978-1-4402-1440-0
Y0237

Edited by Kelly Biscopink
Designed by Kelly O'Dell
Production coordinated by Greg Nock
Photography by Ric Deliantoni and Christine Polomsky
Photo styling by Jen Wilson
Illustrated by Lindsay Quinter

Metric Conversion Chart

To convert	to	multiply by
Inches	Centimeters	2.54
Centimeters	Inches	0.4
Feet	Centimeters	30.5
Centimeters	Feet	0.03
Yards	Meters	0.9
Meters	Yards	1.1

ABOUT THE AUTHOR

Leni Levenson Wiener is a quilter and instructor. She is the author of *Thread Painting* (2007) and *Photo-Inspired Art Quilts* (2009) and her work has been exhibited around the U.S. and internationally. She regularly contributes articles for several art quilt magazines and journals and maintains a blog.

Leni teaches classes and workshops, spanning topics from beginner quilting through both traditional and art quilt techniques.

Please visit www.leniwiener.com for more information or contact Leni at leni@leniwiener.com. She welcomes inquiries about trunk shows, lectures, classes and workshops at your shop or guild.

DEDICATION

This book is dedicated to the generations of women who made beautiful quilts, and to those who keep the tradition alive for future generations.

ACKNOWLEDGMENTS

Thank you to all of the companies that generously supplied materials used in the preparation of this book. (Please see the Resources section on page 126 for more information about the manufacturers who contributed materials.)

I would also like to thank the team at F+W Media: Kelly Biscopink (editor), Kelly O'Dell (designer), Lindsay Quinter (illustrator), Ric Deliantoni and Christine Polomsky (photographers).

Thank you to my family—Fred, Jared and Jordan—and all my friends and students for their continued support.

Table of Contents

Introduction

You've probably thought about it before—how nice it would be to learn to make a quilt. But all those little points and squares may have seemed intimidating, not to mention how old-fashioned some quilt designs look. Well, these are not your grandmother's quilts! They are fresh and modern, quick and easy. These quilts are designed to look more contemporary, and to show off the large-scale prints that are available these days. Because there are no little points to line up, it is easy to be successful from the start.

For those readers who do have quilting experience, these patterns are different than the traditional quilts you have made in the past. For you, these projects will be especially quick and easy and will allow you to relax and have fun with the process.

I have been teaching traditional quilting for years, and although my students are different ages and have different reasons for making their first quilt, one thing is always the same—they want it easy, they want it quick and they want it to look great.

The first thing that makes these quilts easy is that each quilt only requires three fabrics. With easy-to-follow guidelines, you will find the process of fabric selection less intimidating.

Next, you will learn the rotary cutting and strip-piecing method of quilt construction—guaranteed to be faster and more accurate than cutting each individual piece with a template like your grandmother did.

6

Unlike traditional quilt designs, the seams in these quilts do not need to line up perfectly, making it easier for a beginner to complete a quilt that looks artistic and fantastic without lots of pinning or frustration.

Finally, the blocks are large enough that you will not need to make a lot of them in order to put your quilt together. The added benefit of larger blocks is that the fabric you love will really stand out in your finished quilt. All those gorgeous large-scale prints won't get lost in the cutting.

Most of the projects in this book are about 40" (102cm) square and can be used as wall hangings, lap quilts or baby quilts. I always have my beginner students start by making a smaller quilt.

This way, you can successfully finish a quilt in a reasonable amount of time—without taking on an overwhelming project that will end up, unfinished, in a closet. Another advantage to working on a smaller quilt is that the quilting won't be as cumbersome as it can be with a larger project, and you can use a single piece of fabric for the back (no piecing of the quilt back required). Several projects are pictured in a twin-bed size, but all the instructions provide yardage for making both a small-size and a twin-size quilt.

Everything has been designed to allow you to make a great quilt, as easy as 1—2—3!

Making a great quilt means learning to:

THE BASICS

1 USE THE RIGHT TOOLS.
For generations, quilts were made of little pieces of fabric sewn together by hand. But today, with so many great new tools, a quilt goes together in a fraction of the time it took our grandmothers. This section will tell you what tools you need and how to use them.

2 CHOOSE THE RIGHT FABRICS.
Quilters at every level complain that they have a hard time deciding on fabrics, and even when they have chosen their fabrics they don't know where to place them in the quilt. For every quilt project in this book you need only three fabrics. These fabrics are chosen with three criteria—color, value and print scale. Understanding where each fabric works ensures that your quilt will be a **wow**.

3 PUT IT TOGETHER WITH EASY TECHNIQUES.
Cut strips, sew them together, cut them apart, sew them together—it is so easy to make a quilt using strip-piecing methods. Chain piecing and proper pressing make quick work of the quilt top.

It's all here, so let's get started!

Tips From the Author

Start Simple

Experienced quilters will find the projects in this book quick and easy to assemble. But if you have never made a quilt before, you will find the quilts in this book very accessible—there are no seams to line up, the designs are forgiving and the steps are clear and straightforward. Read through all the opening information and instructions, collect your supplies and practice on scraps. Don't be too ambitious for your first project—you will be most successful if you keep it simple and start small. The easiest quilt in this book is SIMPLICI-T (page 48), making it a great one to use as your introduction. When you start with a manageable project, you will gain the confidence for bigger and more complex quilts. Once you get started, you'll be hooked!

Share With Others

A quilt is always a well-received gift—it says warmth, it says comfort, it says love. Don't worry if it isn't perfect. The lucky person who receives a handmade quilt won't notice any imperfections.

Once you finish your quilt, I suggest making a label for the back. A label usually includes the name of the quilter and the year, but it can also include the city you live in and any special information you'd like to include. I have seen lots of beautiful labels on quilts—hand painted, embroidered or embellished, or just a small rectangle of light-colored fabric with the information written in permanent marker. First quilt? Say so on your label. Years from now, someone will want to know who made their cherished quilt.

Enjoy the Process

When you make a quilt yourself, you get to choose the colors and fabrics you love and put them together your way. Don't fret about perfection—relax and enjoy the process. If making a quilt isn't fun, it is just another source of stress in your life. And who needs more stress? Take time for yourself, put on your favorite music and let your quilt-making become a way to unwind and rejuvenate. I hope you enjoy this book and use it to make wonderful quilts and memories!

Tools and Materials

The basic materials and supplies you will need to make a quilt from this book are the same you would use to make almost any quilt or sewing project.

3-FABRIC QUILT NECESSITIES

Tools:

1. A sewing machine in good working condition

2. An iron and ironing surface

3. Rotary cutting tools (cutter, mat, rulers)

Basic sewing supplies:

1. Straight pins (A magnetic pin holder will help keep them together.)

2. Scissors (Designate one pair of scissors for fabric only so they will always be nice and sharp.)

3. Seam ripper (Because we all make a mistake once in a while!)

Materials:

1. Fabric (100% cotton quilting fabric)

2. Thread

3. Needles (Use a new needle in your machine for every new project.)

Finishing supplies:

1. Batting

2. Quilt pins

3. Walking foot

Also helpful:

1. Painter's tape

2. Golden Threads or tracing paper

3. Kwik Klip

SEWING MACHINE

Just like a car, there are basic sewing machines and there are luxury sewing machines. And, like a car, you don't need a top-of-the-line machine to get where you want to go. If your sewing machine hasn't been used for a while, it will need to be oiled and the timing and tension should be checked.

If your machine is not in good working condition, you will spend more time frustrated than you will spend sewing. Nothing can spoil the fun of making a quilt faster than a temperamental machine. So do yourself a favor—take your sewing machine to a qualified technician for a checkup.

IRON

Proper pressing throughout the construction of your quilt is essential. Any iron will do, but I personally like one with steam. If you don't press along the way, your seams will look sloppy and your finished quilt won't look crisp and professional.

ROTARY CUTTING TOOLS

The first step in learning to quilt is learning to rotary cut your fabric.

ROTARY CUTTERS

Rotary cutters come in all shapes and sizes, but they are fundamentally the same. The most important difference is the size of the cutting wheel. Start with a middle-size (45mm) blade; this is the standard size that works best for most cutting projects.

ROTARY CUTTING MATS

Rotary cutting mats come in a variety of sizes and are designed to *heal* when used under a rotary cutter blade. These mats are easily affected by heat, so store your mats flat and away from any heat source. (I put my first cutting mat in the trunk of the car on a warm spring day and then did some errands; it looked like a topographical map by the time I got home!)

   If you have a large, flat storage space away from a radiator or window, feel free to purchase a large cutting mat. For most purposes, you do not need a very large mat since you will be folding the fabric before cutting. Look for a mat 12" × 18" (30cm × 46cm) or larger.

ROTARY CUTTING RULERS

There are so many sizes and types of rotary cutting rulers that I can't even begin to discuss them all, but they fall into three categories:

1. **Rectangle**: The rectangular ruler is the basic rotary ruler that you will need for the projects in this book and for any quilt project you may undertake. These rulers come in many sizes, but I recommend buying one that is 6½" (17cm) wide and at least 12" (30cm) long. I prefer rulers that are marked with a grid of 1" (25mm) squares and with lines every ¼" (6mm). These markings make it very easy to see how many inches you are measuring.

2. **Square**: Square rulers are helpful when *squaring off* blocks to perfect squares. These are good to have for extra assistance, but not as your primary ruler. Square rulers come in lots of sizes, but if you only buy one, I recommend purchasing one that is 16½" (42cm) square. This ruler can be used for any size square from 1" (25mm) up to 16½" (42cm), which will serve you well in most situations. If you want to splurge and buy a second one, I recommend a 6½" (17cm) square ruler. This ruler will be easier to use for squaring smaller blocks.

3. **Specialty**: Specialty rulers usually assist in cutting pieces at odd angles for traditional patterns, and are often specific to a particular quilt design. You will not need any specialty rulers for this book.

12

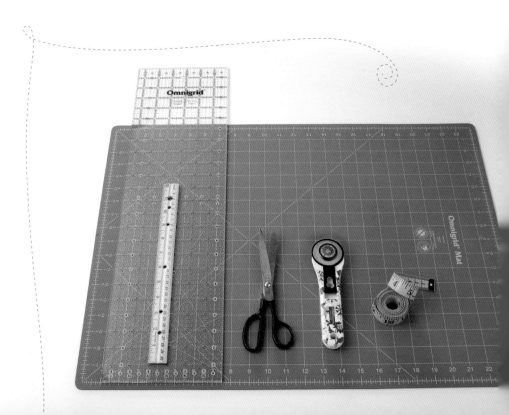

FABRIC

Quilts are most often made from 100 percent cotton fabric. Cotton is the easiest to handle and will not pill over time, like fabrics with acrylic or polyester. Sustainable bamboo fabrics and organic cottons are also available; they are similar to quilting cotton and are environmentally friendly.

Cotton quilting fabric can measure anywhere from 42" to 45" (107cm to 114cm) wide. For that reason, when figuring yardage for this book, I calculate as if the fabric is only 40" (102cm) wide. This allows for little mistakes and differences in fabric widths.

Fabrics purchased in a good quilt shop do not need to be prewashed. In fact, the sizing in the fabric makes it much easier to cut and sew. If you do decide to prewash, wash the fabric with regular detergent and machine dry. Iron all of your prewashed fabric before making your quilt.

There are only three reasons I prewash a fabric:
1. **Discount fabric**: Fabric purchased at a discount store may have a lower thread count and therefore may shrink more than higher quality cottons.
2. **Baby quilts**: I prewash fabric for baby quilts in hot water and a hot dryer so shrinkage will occur before I start cutting and sewing. A busy mom can throw this quilt into the washer and dryer without worrying about special handling. Babies are notoriously unimpressed by handmade quilts and will do all sorts of things to your quilt that will require washing!
3. **Running dye**: Most people expect black and dark blue fabrics to run, but typically it is red dye that is the least stable. Test for colorfastness by putting a corner of each of your fabrics into a saucer of water for 15 to 20 minutes. After this time, any fabric with a thin line of dye running into the water will require prewashing. Do not prewash more than one fabric at a time or you will have a muddled mess. Test the fabric again after prewashing to be sure any dye that wanted to escape has already made its way out.

THREAD

Thread is an important and relatively inexpensive component of your quilt, so resist the urge to purchase bargain thread. Cheap thread can be unevenly spun, and the resulting lumps and thin areas will cause all sorts of problems in the upper tension of your sewing machine.

There are three types of threads used for quilt construction:
1. **Cotton:** Cotton threads are stable and natural, and many quilters like them because they are the same fiber as the fabric. But cotton thread often produces lint that can build up in the bobbin case and in the upper tension wheel.
2. **Polyester:** Polyester thread is strong and stable. It is often thinner than cotton thread, so it will sink into the fabric and more will fit onto a bobbin. Polyester usually produces less lint than cotton.
3. **Poly/cotton:** Poly/cotton blends are strong like polyester and soft like cotton. These blends are also usually the least expensive options.

Ask five quilters what thread they recommend and you will get five different (and impassioned) answers. Any good quality thread will do the job, so try different threads to decide what works best for you and with your sewing machine. When threading your machine, keep in mind that spools are designed to sit straight up and cones should lie horizontally.

I recommend using lingerie thread, thin polyester, or a thread specifically called *bobbin thread* in the bobbin. These threads allow you to get more on the bobbin and work well with any top thread.

Quilts are constructed with a neutral colored thread—there is no need to match your thread to your fabrics. White, medium gray and black threads will satisfy nearly all of your construction needs.

Colored threads can be used for the quilting that shows on the top and bottom of your quilt. You can use a thread that matches a color in the quilt, a thread that contrasts or a variegated thread that changes colors at certain intervals.

BATTING

Batting comes in several varieties:

1. **Cotton:** Cotton batting that is not preshrunk is designed to draw in, giving the quilt an antique look. If this is not what you have in mind, use a cotton batting marked *preshrunk*, or shrink the batting at home. (To preshrink your batting, follow the directions on the label, or place the batting in a tub of hot water for 15 minutes. Then air dry the batting over a shower rod.) Some cotton batting may require denser quilting than poly batting. Many quilters prefer cotton batting because it is a soft and natural fiber.

2. **Polyester:** Polyester battings are usually warmer than cotton battings and come in a wider variety of weights. Polyester batting can require less overall quilt stitching, and it will not shrink.

3. **Poly/cotton blends:** Poly/cotton battings have the feeling of cotton and will not shrink.

4. **Bamboo:** Bamboo batting is environmentally friendly. It performs very much like cotton batting and is indistinguishable from cotton in the finished quilt.

As with threads, most quilters have a personal preference, so try different battings in different projects to decide which you like the best.

Some batting comes with a fusible layer on one or both sides, meaning you can press and fuse it to your quilt rather than pinning. Fusible batting can sometimes pucker over time, so if you use a fusible batting, use one that is fusible on only one side and adhere it to the quilt back.

Batting also comes in a variety of weights:

1. **Traditional:** This relatively thin batting is the most commonly used weight in quilting. Don't confuse the heft of a quilt with that of a down comforter—quilts are meant to be fairly flat so that the quilt stitching shows.

2. **Low-loft:** This weight is thinner than traditional and is suitable for quilted garments, placemats or table toppers.

3. **High-loft:** This weight will make your quilt thick and fluffy. Keep in mind that the higher the loft of the batting, the more cumbersome it will be to quilt.

NEEDLES

Be sure to buy high-quality sewing machine needles and to change the needle in your machine regularly; burrs or nicks on an old needle will cause problems.

Needles come in three types:

1. **Sharp**: designed for use on woven fabrics
2. **Ballpoint**: designed for use on knits to keep the knit from running
3. **Universal**: designed for use on either knit or woven fabrics

Needles also come in various sizes; the proper needle to use with cotton quilt fabric is an 80/12 sharp or universal. Most needles will fit any machine, but if you aren't sure, bring the needle from your machine with you to the quilt shop. Most needles have a flat side at the top, which is usually inserted toward the back of the machine. Refer to your owner's manual for specific information about your machine.

Needles are only good for approximately 5 hours of sewing, so make a habit of changing the needle for every new project.

QUILT PINS

When your quilt is ready to assemble, you will pin all three layers together before quilting. Straight pins will do the job, but they may fall out and can prick your fingers as you work. Quilt pins resemble safety pins with one very important difference—they will not rust.

Regular safety pins are fine if you plan to pin, quilt and remove the pins the same day. But if you leave safety pins in the quilt for even a few days (particularly in damp or humid weather), the pins can rust onto your quilt. These rust spots are difficult (if not impossible) to remove, so it is best to avoid them in the first place.

Quilt pins come in different sizes and shapes. Ultimately, there is not a big difference between them— try a variety to determine which you prefer.

14

KWIK KLIP

The Kwik Klip is a handy little gadget used when pinning your quilt. When inserting your quilt pins, use the grooved point of the Kwik Klip to catch the pin and snap it closed, saving your fingers and your manicure.

PAINTER'S TAPE

The salesmen in my local paint store can't understand why I buy so many rolls of blue painter's tape but I rarely buy paint! Painter's tape is low-tack tape, which means it will not leave a gooey residue. This makes it a great choice for securing your quilt layers while pinning, and for marking guidelines on the quilt top while quilting.

GOLDEN THREADS/TRACING PAPER

There are lots of ways to mark a quilting design onto your quilt, but the method I find consistently effective is to use tracing paper to create a template. Golden Threads is a very thin tracing paper that comes on a roll and is easily torn away after the sewing is done. Regular tracing paper will also do the job, but you may need to tape several sheets together to accomodate the size of the quilting template.

WALKING FOOT

When sewing through two layers of cotton, the feed dogs (the jagged teeth under the sewing machine needle) pull the bottom layer of fabric along in a straight line, and the top layer goes along for the ride. But when you add a layer of batting between them, the bottom fabric is pulled along and the batting and top fabric layers do not move at the same rate, creating puckers and distortions in the quilt.

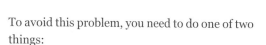

To avoid this problem, you need to do one of two things:
1. Stitch about five to ten stitches, lift and lower the foot, and continue in this way: stitch, lift and lower. It works, but it is time consuming.
2. Use a walking foot. A walking foot is designed to lift and lower with each stitch so that all three layers move along at the same rate. Every sewing machine manufacturer makes a walking foot to fit their machines, or you can buy a generic foot. To purchase a generic, you will need to know if your machine has a high shank, low shank or slanted foot when you go to purchase a generic that will fit. If you aren't sure, bring the entire foot with you (including the "leg") when you go to the quilt shop.

You will notice that the walking foot has either a small bar or a bar with a C attachment. This bar sits on top of the screw that holds the needle in place; the C fits around this screw. When sewing, this screw moves up and down, lifting and lowering the walking foot. If you do not connect this part properly, the foot will not operate differently than any other foot.

Fabric: Color, Value and Print Scale

Even experienced quilters have a hard time choosing their fabrics. For the projects in this book, the process is simplified—you need to choose only three fabrics that meet three criteria: color, value and print scale. In order to make the best choices, you need to understand all three.

COLOR

Most lessons on color are based on a color wheel. After teaching quilters about color over the years, I know that the mere mention of the color wheel is met with glazed stares and lots of shuffling and mumbling. I also find my mind wandering when anyone starts to talk about the physics of color. So you won't find any information in this book about light spectrums or prisms. If you understand the recipes and relationships between colors, you do not need to own, use or think about a color wheel.

PRIMARY COLORS

What I do want you to learn is that every color has a personality, sets a mood and conjures certain emotions. The world is filled with colors, and each one of them elicits a feeling.

Let us start with the basics. There are three primary colors. You have certainly heard this before, but what exactly does it mean? Simple. There are only three colors from which all other colors are made.

You probably already know that the three primary colors are red, blue and yellow. If you come to understand these three colors, you will understand the recipes used for the creation of all other colors, and why and how they relate to each other.

You may be thinking that black and white are also primary colors. Technically, they are not colors at all. Here is that physics again—black is the absence of all color and white the presence of all color. (Here ends the physics lesson.) We will discuss the impact of black and white in a bit. For now, let's begin by looking at the three primary colors—red, blue and yellow.

Name: Red
Type: one of three primary colors
Personality: bold, warm, fiery, passionate
Plays well with: oranges and purples
Opposite: green
Mood: hot and passionate
Range: from deep maroon to petal pink

Name: Blue
Type: one of three primary colors
Personality: cool, calm
Plays well with: greens and purples
Opposite: orange
Mood: serene and tranquil
Range: from navy to baby blue

Name: Yellow
Type: one of three primary colors
Personality: warm, sunny
Plays well with: oranges and greens
Opposite: purple
Mood: happy
Range: from bright to light

Remember when you were in kindergarten and got your hands into the finger paint? You learned the first basic recipes when you started moving your fingers around the paper:

red + yellow = orange

red + blue = purple

blue + yellow = green

When you swirled the paint around and the red, yellow and blue got mixed together, it made brown.

When black is added to any color, it gets darker. The more black you add, the darker the color. This is called a *shade*. When white is added to any color, it gets lighter. The more white you add, the lighter the color. This is called a *tint*.

Now, let's look at how colors play together.

COMPLEMENTARY COLORS

Complementary (or opposite) colors will seem to visually vibrate when put together. Understanding color complements allows you to bring excitement and energy to your quilts. Placement of a complementary color can draw attention to a certain area of a quilt, or create a secondary design.

You probably already know the basic complementary colors, but if you understand *why* they are complements, you will be able to establish what the complements are for more complex colors, without the need of the confusing color wheel.

If you mix blue and yellow together to make green, the leftover primary is red—the complementary color of green. Mixing yellow and red makes orange; the remaining primary, and therefore the complement, is blue. Mixing red and blue makes purple; the remaining primary and complement is yellow.

Using just a small amount of a complementary color in an assortment will add a bit of pizzazz to your quilt. Using equal amounts can be visually overwhelming.

So what about more nuanced colors? Let's use the example of teal, a combination of blue and green. We know that the complement of blue is orange and the complement of green is red. Therefore, the complement to teal is a red-orange. If there is more blue in the teal, the complement will be more orange-red; if there is more green in the teal, the complement will be more red-orange.

Brown (all three primaries mixed together) and gray (white and black mixed together) can each have an underlying *agenda*. A true gray is equal parts of white and black, but not all grays are true grays—some have blue in them, some have yellow and some red; this means they will each look gray but with a tint of another color. The same holds true for brown—if there is more yellow in the mix, the resulting brown will look different than if there is more red in it. Mixing brown and gray together will give you taupe, and the amount of each color in that mix will also give you an underlying color.

These gray and brown variations can be confusing, but sometimes the easiest way to determine a color's underlying agenda is to hold it next to a red, a blue and a yellow to see which color it most closely matches. Once you have identified the recipe in the brown, gray or taupe, it will be easier to find other fabrics that will work well with it, and which color will be the most effective complement.

If you look at any color and break down its recipe, it is easy to figure out exactly which other color will give it that complementary spark.

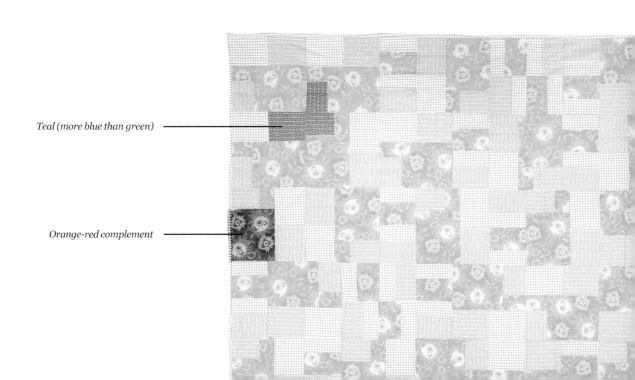

Teal (more blue than green)

Orange-red complement

COLOR TEMPERATURE

Blues and greens are cool colors—the colors of water and plants. They set a mood that is quiet and serene, restful and natural. Reds and oranges, on the other hand, are warm colors—the colors of fire and heat, passion and energy. Purple can play on either team. Understanding the *temperature* of the colors you choose will allow you to set the mood of your quilt.

Mixing warm and cool colors, even if they are not true complementary colors, can give your quilt a visual jolt. Mixing them together in equal amounts will result in a quilt that looks jarring and jumbled. Mixing in a small amount of cool color to your warm assortment, or vice versa, can bring all the colors to life.

SATURATION

Another aspect of color that can change the mood is *saturation*. Think of saturation like dye—a bit of blue dye on white fabric will yield a soft baby blue (lightly saturated). Leave the white fabric in blue dye for a long time and the color becomes deep and rich (more highly saturated).

Just as with color alone, if you add white to a saturated color, it gets lighter. Add black and it gets darker. But if you add both white and black, the color becomes *dusty*, or grayer. The grayer a color becomes, the less saturation it has.

Highly saturated colors feel tropical and bright; lower saturated colors feel soft, romantic and maybe a little antique.

For juvenile quilts, saturated primary colors combined with complementary colors will result in a quilt with lots of energy and visual excitement.

Baby quilts, where energy and excitement is not the goal, are better in a single, less saturated color range like yellow, blue or pink. Mixing these colors with white (instead of complementary color accents) will result in a quilt that is more soothing.

Using white in your quilt will make colors look crisp and clear; black will intensify colors around it. Beige will make your quilt look antique and feminine, and will work better with less saturated, grayer colors like dusty rose, lilac and soft sage green.

COLOR SCHEMES

The three basic color combinations are:

1. **Monochromatic**: a color scheme built of a single color. A single color quilt will have a quiet dignity. Adding white to a single color will make it appear crisp and fresh; adding black to a single color will look more dramatic. Monochromatic color schemes are easy to manage and always look well balanced. Since there is no contrast from color, value is extremely important for a successful monochromatic quilt.

2. **Analogous**: a color scheme built of two or more colors adjacent to each other on the color wheel. Don't panic! This usually means using either cools or warms—blues/greens/yellows, reds/oranges/yellows or reds/blues/purples. An analogous color scheme will appear more complex than a monochromatic color scheme, but with the same serenity.

3. **Complementary**: a color scheme that includes the complementary color of the predominant color in the assortment. Adding at least one complementary color will give a spark of life to the quilt. In a quilt with only three fabrics, use one complement and the color proportions will always be correct. A complementary color is most effective when used to highlight a design element in the quilt and when used in a different value (see page 19). Not sure about the complement? Use a warm color with a cool assortment and a cool color with a warm assortment.

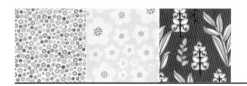

VALUE

Value can be as, or even more important than color alone. No matter how sophisticated your understanding of color, your results will fall flat without understanding the simple rules of value.

Value is the light, medium and dark of the fabrics in your assortment. Value is relative—a fabric that is light in one quilt may be medium or dark in another. Most of us tend to be attracted to fabrics that fall in the same midvalue range. It is important to include lighter and darker fabrics to round out the assortment. When buying fabrics for a project, the potential candidates must be compared to each other to be certain that there are light, medium and dark values included.

If the colors you choose include a range of values, the quilt will have contrast and will look lively and exciting. Leave out the light and dark, and the colors will blend together and fall flat. This is also true for using all light values or all dark values. No contrast means no excitement.

Often the values of fabrics can be seen with the naked eye, but there are situations where you might benefit from using a red viewer. This is a small piece of red plastic though which to view your fabrics. The red cancels out colors so you can only perceive values. You can instantly tell if the fabrics are light, medium or dark tones, without being distracted by colors. But when choosing only three fabrics for a quilt, as we will be doing for these projects, the values should be easily identified with the naked eye.

When choosing complementary colors, remember that they do not need to be the same value. Whether a color is lighter or darker does not change its complement. In fact, changing the values of complementary colors can make your color combination more successful. A quilt that is primarily green would benefit from the addition of a small amount of red, but for a less jarring and equally effective spark of color use pink, the lighter value of red.

PRINT SCALE

Any fabric that is not a solid color has a small-, medium- or large-scale pattern on it. Like value, *scale* is relative—what may be a small-scale print in one fabric assortment could be medium in another. Density also affects the way print scale appears; some prints are closely packed, while others have lots of background showing through. This can change the scale of the print as well as the appearance of the value.

Antique quilts are distinguished by the use of small-scale calico prints. For more than one hundred years, quilters did not have many choices when it came to print scale. Using only small prints will give your quilt an old-fashioned look.

In recent years, larger scale prints are appearing in quilt shops. Even traditional patterns made in large-scale fabrics will look more modern and updated. When deciding on the placement of your fabrics, it is important to establish where the largest areas of the quilt are so that the beautiful large-scale print is not lost by being cut into small pieces. (The patterns in this book will direct you where to use your largest scale print.)

Just as variations in value and color will make a quilt more dynamic, variations in scale will, too. All of these factors combine to create layers of complexity that make the overall quilt look more interesting and nuanced. When choosing your three fabrics, think about selecting one small-scale print, one medium-scale print and one large-scale print.

Now you are ready to pick out your fabric!

Small Scale   Medium Scale   Large Scale

Choosing 3 Fabrics

START WITH A FOCUS FABRIC

The process of selecting fabrics most often begins with a single fabric. Your starting fabric will set the mood and style of your quilt and establish your color scheme. Using the colors in this starting fabric is the easiest way to build an assortment of fabrics. Everything else is built on this foundation.

You will choose three fabrics for your quilt, remembering to keep three things in mind: color, value and print scale.

Always begin your fabric search by locating one fabric you love. Maybe you have a specific room in mind, so you would match your fabrics to the colors in that room. Maybe you have a favorite color. Look around the fabric shop and choose a fabric that speaks to you. This is your *focus fabric*.

In choosing this focus fabric, look for one with many colors and a specific feeling or style. Often this starting point is the largest scale print in the assortment, but it doesn't have to be. It should, however, establish the colors that will be in the final quilt. While searching for your starting fabric, you may fall in love with a beautiful subtle single-color fabric with a small scale—hold on to it for use as a supporting player, but resist trying to use it as your starting point.

CHOOSE TWO COORDINATING FABRICS

Fabric designers are well educated in color theory, so take advantage of their knowledge. Using the colors in the fabric as a guide will make your finished quilt as effective as this fabric you love.

Many fabrics have a print key for the screen printing on the selvage. This is usually a row of circles showing each individual color printed on the white selvage. Although not all fabrics have this guide, those that do provide a clear map of colors to look for when choosing coordinating fabrics. But remember, those you choose do not need to be the same value.

It would be easy to simply match solid fabrics to each of these colors, but the resulting quilt would have no particular excitement. Choose one coordinating/complementary color at a time, and look at potential fabric candidates.

Look for fabrics that have more than one of the colors in the starting fabric. This will make the assortment more interesting and exciting. If your coordinating fabric has additional colors in it, don't pass it up. As long as everything works together, it will add interest to your assortment.

When choosing candidates, it is important to think about the style of the starting fabric, not just the colors. Is your focus fabric soft and romantic? Is it hard-edged and graphic? Is it whimsical and childlike? Does it look retro? Fabrics that work best together will have similar attributes to your focus fabric. If the colors are right but the style is different, the result won't be a *wow*.

As you narrow your selection, your decisions will become more focused and subtle. Does one fabric have more of the focus colors than another? Are two of them too similar? Are the print scales different? Would a stripe be more interesting than another geometric? Does the assortment need something that reads like a solid to calm things down and give the eye a chance to rest? Would a color be better in a different value? Thinking now about the placement of your fabrics in the final quilt will also help you make these decisions.

Some manufacturers put together a line of coordinating fabrics, usually merchandised together in the store. I find that most of these coordinating fabrics, although beautiful, are often very close to each other in value or print scale. If this is the case, pick one fabric that you love from the line, and go searching for two coordinating fabrics that will be a better match, remembering that light/medium/dark values and large-/medium-/small-print scales will give the best result.

Fabrics

USING BLACK AND WHITE

A very easy way to choose three fabrics is to start with black and white. Thinking back to value, remember that black will be the darkest value and white the lightest, so just about anything you put with black and white will look good. Some black-and-white print fabrics are predominately black, others predominately white; choose one of each and add one more color—smashing! When building an assortment this way, remember to choose one small-, one medium- and one large-scale print.

BACKING FABRIC

Finally, all the projects in this book list the backing fabric as a separate yardage. If you plan to use the quilt on a bed, you may want to use one of the three main fabrics on the back. If you plan to hang the quilt on the wall, you can choose a less expensive solid cotton, since no one will see the back anyway.

This may seem like a complicated process, but if your fabrics don't look great together, all your careful work will not yield the results you want.

3-Fabric Tip

Since most quilt shops organize their fabrics by color, I find that holding the starting fabric up to one color area is a quick and easy way to spot the fabrics that should be pulled off the shelf for further evaluation. Looking at the bolt edge allows you to see how the fabrics will look when cut up and reassembled. It is always better to pull a lot of fabrics and eliminate them than to keep going back to the shelf for more fabric.

3-Fabric Tip

There are lots of gorgeous batik fabrics available these days. Some are patterned and some read like solids with interesting variations of color or value in them. These batiks are great to use, provided they match the style of your other fabrics.

If you are using fabrics that look like watercolor paintings, or are soft and pretty, batiks will be a great addition to your assortment. If you are using strong, clean-line graphic fabrics, the batik may look mismatched.

COMPARING AND SELECTING FABRICS

 This floral is the focus fabric. I was attracted to the bright, cheerful, saturated colors. The fabric has lots of movement, and there are many colors to choose coordinates from in the print.

 Green 1 is a tone-on-tone floral that works nicely with the colors in the focus fabric. The scale is smaller and the print is similar in style, making it a nice option.

 Green 2 has swirls, which look nice with the flowing shapes in the focus fabric. The green and gold tones relate nicely to the tones in the focus fabric. The scale, however, is very close to the scale of the floral.

 Green 3 is a geometric that is a nice counterpoint to the floral. The scale is good, and I like the addition of turquoise and off-white that are also in the focus fabric. Another nice option.

 Yellow 1 looks great with the focus fabric. It is similar in print, the scale works and it looks bright and cheerful.

 Yellow 2 almost works since the color and print are good, but the scale is too close to the scale of the focus fabric.

 Blue 1 is just slightly off in color, although it is close enough to work if I find other fabrics that coordinate well. Scale and value are good.

 Blue 2 is dark and saturated, and relates nicely to the dark blue in the focus fabric. The scale is good, but it feels a little too strong and might overpower the focus fabric.

 Blue 3 is a small-scale turquoise-on-turquoise print. The dark and light tones and the leaf print relate nicely to the floral. It could work, with the right partner.

 Blue 4 is a turquoise daisy print with yellow centers. I like this color combination, the scale works and the color is bright, saturated and dramatic.

 Pink 1 is great with the focus fabric; the strong dark color is a nice contrast. The very small scale reads almost like a solid, giving the eye a resting place next to the more complex focus fabric.

 Pink 2 could work—the colors and scale work well with the focus fabric.

 Pink 3 is a smaller scale floral than the focus fabric. The dark pink and the similar-looking print look good with the focus fabric.

POTENTIAL COMBINATIONS

FOCUS FABRIC + BLUE 4 + YELLOW 1
I like the scale and the colors, but the two prints are so similar that they become redundant.

FOCUS FABRIC + BLUE 4 + PINK 2
This is better; color, scale and print all work, but the blue and pink are a bit too close in value.

FOCUS FABRIC + BLUE 4 + PINK 3
Nope! Too similar in pattern, too close in scale and too close in value.

FOCUS FABRIC + BLUE 3+ YELLOW 1
The two additional prints are too close in scale and in value—not a good combination.

FOCUS FABRIC + BLUE 4 + PINK 1
This is the best so far; colors work well, as do the scale. I am a bit concerned that the values are too close, although they are not the same.

FOCUS FABRIC + PINK 1 + GREEN 1
Not bad! The green and pink are different values as well as complementary colors, so this works.

FOCUS FABRIC + PINK 1 + YELLOW 1
The yellow is a bit brighter and more cheerful than Green 1. The scale of the fabrics, the pattern styles, and the colors all complement each other in a way that makes this my favorite option.

Your final choices may be different, but remember to consider:
Color
Scale
Value
Arc the prints compatible?

Rotary Cutting

Rotary cutting is the fastest and most accurate way to cut your fabrics and begin your quilt. Get into the habit of closing the blade after every cut. Even a blade that is too dull to cut fabric can do a very good job on fingers! If you aren't getting a clean cut, you may need a new blade.

When you purchase cotton quilting fabric, your yardage will be folded in the center, as it was on the bolt. If you open up your piece of fabric, you will see that the two outside edges are tightly woven to prevent unraveling. These tightly woven edges are called the *selvages*. The selvage is often white with the name of the manufacturer and a color key printed on it. Sometimes it is the same color or print as the rest of the fabric.

To begin rotary cutting, fold the fabric in half so that the two selvages line up. This is often the same way it was folded on the bolt, but not always. Lining up the selvages will ensure that your fabric will be cut on the *straight of grain* and the strips will be straight. You cannot be certain the fabric has been cut off the bolt at a right angle to the selvages, so it is important to align the selvages so the rest of the fabric falls flat without buckling.

Once you have lined up your selvages and the fabric folds nicely in half, fold the fabric in half again, bringing the folded edge to meet the selvage edge. Now you have a shorter distance to cut and everything will be straight. If this step isn't done carefully, you will get strips that undulate.

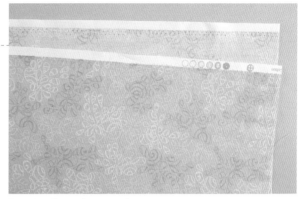

Locate the selvage edges.

Fold fabric in half, and in half again.

Note: Rotary cutting is different if you are right- or left-handed. These instructions are right-handed; if you are left-handed you will need to start cutting on the opposite side.

3-Fabric Tip

Accurate cutting means accurate sewing, so be slow and thoughtful while cutting your strips.

The three most important things to remember about rotary cutting are:
1. Always cut away from you.
2. Always close the blade after every cut.
3. Always keep your rotary cutter away from children.

24

The first cut you make is called the *square-off cut*. This cut establishes a nice straight edge, ensuring all strips will be perfectly straight. The square-off cut must be at a right angle to the folded edge of your fabric.

Lay the folded piece of fabric onto the cutting mat so that the edge you plan to cut first (for your square-off cut) is on the right. Put your ruler along this cut edge, lined up with the narrowest spot. Make sure that the lines on the ruler are aligned with the folded edges of the fabric, so that the cut you make is at a right angle to the fold and the selvage.

With your left hand, hold the ruler firmly in place, making sure your fingers don't hang over the edge of the ruler. With your right hand, unlock the rotary cutter and, starting on the cutting mat just before the fabric starts, make one hard, clean cut, pressing the blade edge against the right edge of the ruler. Put your weight into it so that you can do this in one motion; sawing back and forth will only make a mess of your fabric. Now you have a clean cut that is perpendicular to the folds of the fabric.

Since the edges of the fabric on all layers are neatly lined up, you don't want to move the fabric and disturb the even edges. Turn the mat so that the newly cut side is now on your left. If you are working on a small table, you can also move to the opposite side of the table. It is important, however, not to lift the fabric to turn it.

Now you are ready to cut your strips. Let's say you are cutting a 3" (8cm) strip. Slide the ruler so that the 3" (8cm) mark is on the edge of your fabric; this means 3" (8cm) of the ruler will overlap onto your fabric. In the same way you made your square-off cut, cut against the right edge of the ruler, starting the cut on the mat just before the fabric. If you have multiple strips to cut, simply move that strip away and continue along until you have the number of strips you need.

Note: A left-handed quilter will do the cutting in the same way, except that the square-off cut will be done on the left and then all subsequent cuts will be made from the right. A left-handed person will cut with the blade against the left edge of the ruler.

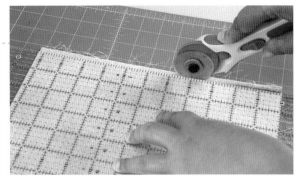
Make the square-off cut.

Rotate your cutting mat, align your ruler and cut your first strip.

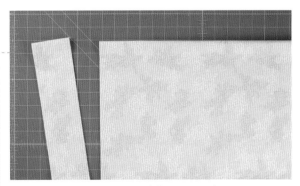
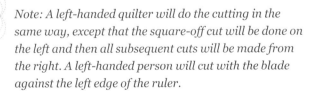
Move your first strip out of the way and continue to cut strips until finished.

TIPS ON ROTARY CUTTING

1. If you have multiple strips the same width to cut (even if they are from different fabrics), use a sticky note or a piece of painter's tape to mark that line on your ruler. That way you won't have to find the line for every strip you cut. Use a pen to draw an arrow on the tape to indicate the correct edge in order to avoid confusion.

2. Even though the mat has a cutting grid on it, I ignore it and rely on the ruler. There are times when we will make use of the mat grid, but not now. If it confuses you, flip the mat over to the plain side. This will also help you get longer life out of your mat.

3. If you go off course and end up with an uneven cut, turn the mat and do another square-off cut—just like you did when you started. Then rotate the mat again and continue cutting strips.

4. If you are cutting multiple strips from a fabric and do not plan to cut them all at the same time, put three pins into the cut end of the folded fabric. This way, you will not have to make another square-off cut when you return to this fabric.

26

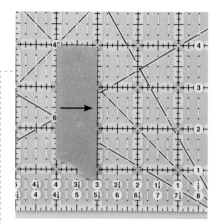

Mark a frequent measurement on your ruler with painter's tape.

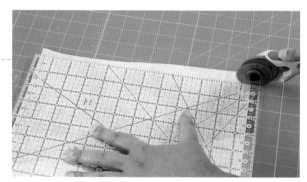

If your fabric gets uneven, square off the edge.

Place three pins in the cut end of the folded fabric.

ROTARY CUTTING STRIPS LARGER THAN YOUR RULER

OK, you took my advice and purchased a rotary ruler that is 6½" (17cm) wide, but now my instructions call for strips wider than 6½" (17cm). So, what do you do?

When the strip to be cut is wider than the ruler, do your square-off cut in the usual way.

You then have two options for cutting strips:
1. Line up the fabric with the grid on your cutting mat—be sure to line up the top and the side so that you know the cut strips will be straight. Then use the ruler to cut, using the grid lines on the mat as your measurement. The grid is marked in 1" (3cm) squares, so measuring is pretty simple.
2. Use two rulers to add up the amount you need to measure. For example, if you need a 7½" (19cm) strip and have a 6½" (17cm) ruler, use another ruler to add 1" (2cm) to the edge.

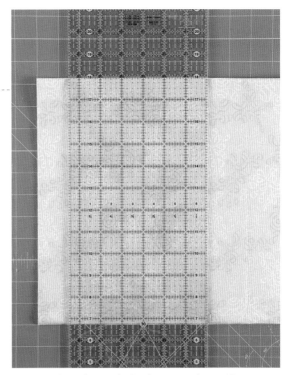

Line up the ruler with the lines on the grid.

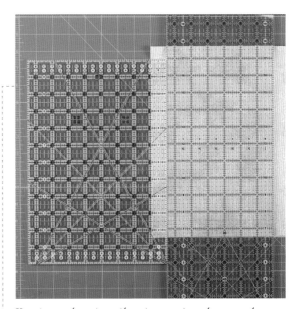

Use two rulers together to create a larger ruler.

Strip Piecing and Construction Methods

Not long ago, quilts were made by cutting each individual piece of fabric with a template and a pair of scissors. This was not only very time-consuming, it was not terribly accurate. Quilts were constructed by sewing those little pieces together one at a time.

Now, the fastest and easiest way to construct a quilt is with a method called *strip piecing*. Strip piecing is fun, and the results are more accurate than template sewing for some patterns.

In this method, strips are sewn together in a particular order and then cut apart into blocks or parts of blocks. These blocks are rearranged and sewn into a quilt top. This method allows you to put together a quilt in a very short period of time.

The instructions for each individual quilt will indicate how wide to cut your strips, what order to sew the strips together and how wide to cut the strip sets apart. Although the principle remains the same, the results can be very different. Refer to the specific instructions for the quilt you want to make to see how to strip piece your quilt.

SETTING UP THE MACHINE

Before you begin to sew, make sure that your stitch length and tension are properly set. Many new machines have self-adjusting tension and a default standard stitch length. Your stitch length should be about eight to ten stitches per inch, or 2.5 to 3 on machines set up from 1 to 6.

Balanced tension means that the top and bottom threads intersect to form stitches that look perfect on both the top and bottom of the sewn fabric. If the bobbin thread seems to come to the surface in loops, turn your tension number to a lower number and try again. If the top thread is looping or bunching up on the bottom of your work, the tension needs to be set at a higher number. Remember this rule: *if the bobbin thread comes up, turn the number down.* Do not attempt to make changes to your bobbin tension by tightening or loosening the screw on the bobbin case; this is something only a qualified technician should adjust.

USING ¼" (6MM) SEAM ALLOWANCE

A seam allowance is the distance from the edge of the fabric to the stitches. For quilts, ¼" (6mm) is the standard seam allowance.

There are several ways to measure and maintain the ¼" (6mm) seam allowance:

1. **Quarter-inch foot**:
   The distance from the edge of this special sewing machine foot to the needle is exactly ¼" (6mm). Keep the edge of the foot aligned with the edge of your fabric to maintain the right seam allowance at all times.

2. **Adjustable needle position**: Newer sewing machines offer the ability to move the needle from the center of the foot to either the right or left. Depending on your machine, the right needle position may be ¼" (6mm) from the edge of the foot. If so, adjust your needle position and use your standard sewing foot in the same way you would use a quarter-inch foot.

3. **Marking the sewing machine**: Using your standard sewing foot, place your rotary ruler under the foot, positioned so that the needle is directly over the first ¼" (6mm) line from the edge. The right edge of the ruler is now exactly ¼" (6mm) from the needle. Use a permanent marker or painter's tape to mark the edge of the ruler onto the

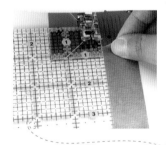

sewing machine. When you line up the edge of your fabric with this line, you will be sewing a ¼" (6mm) seam allowance.

BASIC STRIP-PIECING INSTRUCTIONS

There are three basic methods of strip piecing, all of which will be used in the projects in this book:

1. Sewing strips together and cutting them apart
2. Adding pieced units to a strip of fabric
3. Chain piecing sewn units together

SEWING STRIPS TOGETHER

The instructions for every quilt will tell you which strips to sew together in which order, and how to cut them apart. Following the specific instructions for the quilt you plan to make, take two strips to be sewn together and place them face to face, or *right sides together*.

Although the selvage edge will not remain in our finished quilt, do not cut it off. Instead, place the strips so that the selvage lies just past the hole in the machine where the bobbin thread comes up. This will prevent the corner of your fabric from being pulled down when you begin to sew. Unlike other kinds of sewing, there is no need to backstitch at the beginning and end of your strips.

Make sure that the right-hand edges of your two strips are lined up accurately. There is no need to pin these strips. Make any adjustments as you sew, keeping the right edges aligned at all times and maintaining a ¼" (6mm) seam allowance. Don't push or pull your fabric through the machine, which can stretch or distort the fabric; let the feed dogs do the work for you. Use your right hand to keep the edges of the strips together and your left hand to gently guide them through at the ¼" (6mm) mark.

Sew all the way to the end of the strips. Don't be alarmed if one is longer than the other—not all 45" (114cm) wide fabric is really 45" (114cm), so your strips could be different by several inches. Remember that all the instructions in this book assume a width of only 40" (102cm), allowing for any inconsistency in the fabric width.

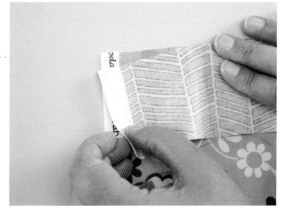

Place two strips right sides together.

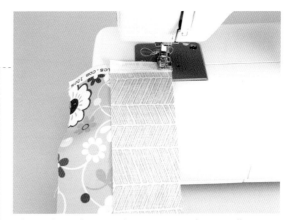

Place the selvage edge just past the needle.

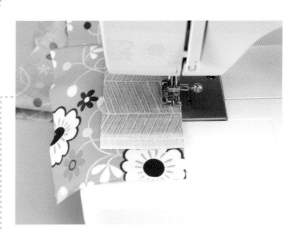

Sew to the end of the strips. Don't worry if the ends are uneven.

PRESSING

After each set of strips is sewn, it is important to press the seams for neat and accurate results. After each seam is complete, it must be pressed in three steps:

1. **Press as sewn**: Pressing is not a back-and-forth movement like ironing. Simply put the iron down onto the finished seam, lift and move to the next section until the whole seam is pressed. The heat allows the fabric to relax and makes the seam look flat with no puckers.

2. **Press to one side**: Seams in quilts are usually pressed to one side or the other. In most cases, the instructions will tell you in which direction to press. The primary reason for pressing to one side is so that when one block is sewn to another the seams will interlock, allowing you to skip pinning.

3. **Press from the top**: This final step is very important for accuracy. When you flip the strip over with the right side up, you may see that in pressing your seam allowance to one side, the front has a *rollover* that needs to be flattened. Place the iron on the quilt next to the rollover area and slide the iron over the rollover, pressing it flat.

From the back, press the seam to one side.

Press from the top, flattening the rollover.

CUTTING THE STRIP SET INTO UNITS

Now that your strip set is complete, the quilt instructions will tell you how to cut it apart. Just as you did when you began cutting your strips, square off one end of your strip set. This will remove the selvage and give you a nice clean edge to start cutting.

Lay the strip on the cutting mat and use the ruler to cut an even starting point. When cutting strips, line up the ruler marks with the seam lines so you can be sure you are cutting straight. Remember that the seams are now a permanent part of your quilt, so even if the raw edges are not straight, you must use the seams as your guide. Make the cuts as you move across the strip according to the specific instructions.

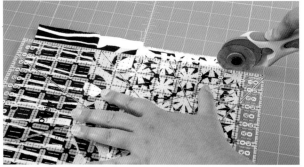

Square one end of the strip set.

Cut the strip set into units.

ADDING PIECED UNITS TO ANOTHER STRIP

After you create your strip sets and cut the units, you may be instructed to add this unit of pieced fabric to another strip.

To do this, place the strip of fabric right-side-up in the machine. Then, in the direction indicated, place one unit right-side-down onto this strip with the right-hand edges lined up. Sew down the right-hand edge with a ¼" (6mm) seam allowance until you reach the end of this unit. Place another unit directly below the first and continue sewing until all the units have been added to the strip.

These will be pressed open and cut apart to form even more complex units.

COMBINING UNITS AND CHAIN PIECING

Once two different units are completed, they are often combined into the final quilt block. The fastest way to do this is by chain piecing.

When sewing units together to create blocks, you could sew one, pull it out of the machine, cut the thread and move on to the next. But this is not the most efficient way to piece these blocks. Chain piecing can save you time and thread.

To begin chain piecing two units together, make a pile of the first unit all in the same direction. Repeat with a pile of the second unit. Position these next to your sewing machine so that they are in the correct positions to pick up, flip one on top of the other and sew together.

Stitch the first set, making sure to maintain ¼" (6mm) seam allowance. When you have reached the end of the block, feed the next set under the needle, allowing the blocks to be connected by a thin line of thread. Spacing them approximately ¼" (6mm) apart will prevent accidentally sewing them together. At the end of the chain, remove all the blocks from the machine, cut the threads apart and you will have all your finished blocks ready to press and continue.

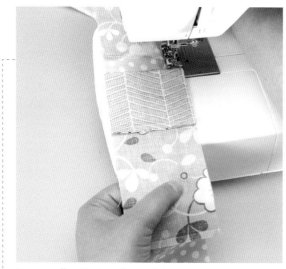

Sew small units to a long strip.

Chain piece units together.

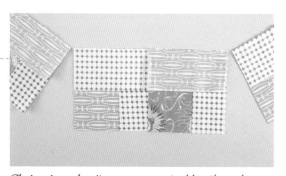

Chain pieced units are connected by thread.

SQUARING OFF THE BLOCKS

Once your blocks are completed, check them to see if they are straight. If you have sewn carefully, there may be no need to trim your blocks at all.

Squaring off is most easily accomplished with a large square ruler. Place the square ruler onto the block so that the upper-right corner of the block is aligned with the upper-right corner of the ruler. Locate the lines on the ruler that indicate the size block you want—for example, 8½" (22cm)—and place the ruler lines at 8½" (22cm) on the bottom and the left side of the block. Trim the right edge and top. Now turn the block 180 degrees so that the cut edges are in the form of an L. Repeat the process for the two uncut sides. Make sure all horizontal and vertical seams in the block line up with the lines in the ruler before you cut.

If you do not have a square ruler, line up the block with the grid on your mat. Use your rotary ruler to trim one side at a time.

LAYING OUT THE BLOCKS

The quilts in this book are designed to allow you to put the quilt together any way you would like. You can put all the blocks in the same direction if you want a symmetrical balance to your quilt top, or arrange them randomly to give your quilt a more contemporary look. There is no right or wrong way; it is all up to you. Determine the layout of your quilt by laying the blocks on a table, a bed or the floor.

Even for a random arrangement of blocks, I do not leave the arrangement completely to chance. I prefer to do something I call a *controlled random*. Controlled random means that, although the block arrangement looks completely random, the blocks are placed in a balanced way that allows the eye to move across the surface of the quilt.

I do this by paying attention to either one color or shape, or the orientation of each block, and placing the blocks so that nothing looks clumped together. Often I move the blocks around like puzzle pieces, stepping back and evaluating before coming to a final decision about what looks visually pleasing.

Square up the block using a large, square ruler.

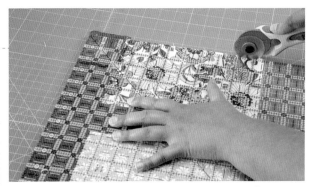

Trim up one side of the ruler and then across the top.

3 Steps to Accurate Piecing

When creating a strip-pieced quilt, there are three things to think about:

1. Accurate rotary cutting
2. Maintaining a ¼" (6mm) seam allowance
3. Pressing

If your strips are cut accurately, the seam allowance is consistent and the seams are pressed as you go, the quilt will go together beautifully and without a hitch. But remember as you work that, like anything else, the more you do this, the better you will be at it. If everyone could make a perfect, prizewinning quilt the first time they tried, where would the challenge be? Why would you ever want to make a second one? So enjoy the process and learn as you go.

PINNING AND SEWING BLOCKS TOGETHER

According to the quilt instructions, you will now sew your blocks together to form the quilt top. Usually this is done in rows, but in some cases it is done in sections. Typically, it makes no difference in what order the blocks are sewn together.

Once the layout is determined, leave the blocks in position, and one row at a time, pin the blocks together so their position doesn't change. Pinning your pieces to sew is not always necessary. Some people want their sewing as close to perfect as possible, and some are more go-with-the-flow types. If you choose to pin for greater accuracy, there are a few rules that will help make it easy.

Accuracy does not require many pins—one at the beginning of a section, one around the middle and one toward the end is enough. Too many pins can distort your fabric, actually making your sewing less accurate.

Always pin perpendicular to the seam you plan to sew, rather than pinning on the seam line. The head of the pin should be on the left, with the point of the pin toward the seam to be sewn. This serves two purposes: First, it will allow you to easily pull the pin out as it approaches the sewing needle. This is important as you never want to sew over a pin. In the battle between needle and pin, it is the needle that will break, and if you are sewing fast enough, you can also damage your machine.

Pointing the tip of the pin toward the seam to be sewn will also remind you where you were planning to sew in case you are interrupted. If the phone rings, someone needs you or the rice is boiling over, you can leave your work and come back to it later. When the pin points to the seam to be sewn, you will never need to figure out where you intended to sew, even if you don't come back to it for a long time.

Once you have pinned your rows together, pin a piece of paper to mark the first block of each row with the row number. This will help you put all the rows together without getting confused.

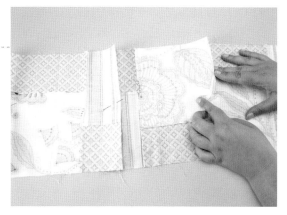

Pin all blocks in a row together.

The pin tip should point toward the seam.

Remove pins as you reach them—don't sew over them!

33

SEWING ROWS TOGETHER

As you put together your rows of blocks, pinning can be very helpful for lining up seams. Although there are no points to match in the construction of the blocks in these quilts, you may want to accurately piece where the blocks come together from one row to the next. This requires a pin—and only one pin—per intersection.

When sewing the rows of blocks together, press the seam allowances on the odd-numbered rows in one direction and the even-numbered rows in the other. This ensures that the seam allowances will interlock when the rows are placed right sides together for sewing.

Lay the intersection of the two blocks right sides together. With your fingers, feel how these seam allowances seem to lock together. If you want to be certain these intersections do not shift while sewing, use a pin to lock them in place. With the blocks right sides together and the seams locked, place a pin into the seam, through the block beneath and up into the seam again. Flip the blocks over and make sure the pin goes through the seam on the back. Gently slide the pin out as your needle reaches it while sewing.

Once all the rows are sewn together in order, your quilt top is complete.

SQUARING OFF THE QUILT TOP

Once the top of the quilt is sewn together, it needs to be pressed well and squared off one final time before layering and quilting. The quilt top is now larger than your mat, so look at one section at a time and make sure that the edges are straight and the corners are square.

Look for areas that seem to jut in or out and use a ruler to determine where they should lie. If the jut is out, use the ruler to trim that area off; if it juts in, make sure that the seam allowance will absorb it (see page 45 for more information about absorbing shortages and blocking). It is helpful to use existing seams in the quilt as a ruler guide.

34

Opposing seam allowances will interlock.

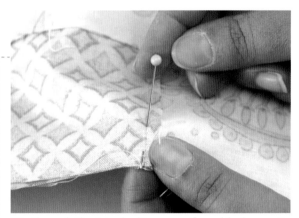

Pin through the interlocking seam for added security.

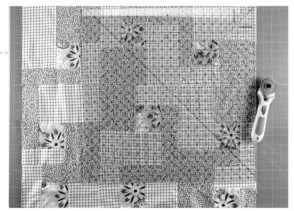

Square off the quilt top with a large, square ruler.

Finishing Your Quilt

Now that your quilt top is complete, it is time to put the three quilt layers together. A quilt is defined as having a front/top (usually pieced), a middle batting layer and a quilt back, all held together with stitching. This stitching, or quilting, can be functional or decorative, and the thread can be an accent color or can blend unnoticed.

The final step is to encase the edges of a quilt with a fabric binding. Since the edges of a quilt take the most wear and tear, the binding protects the edges of your quilt and gives it a pretty frame. Although there are other ways to finish a quilt, most are finished with a binding edge.

PREPARING THE QUILT BACK

If you are making a quilt that is less than 45" (114cm) in one direction, you will not need to piece the back fabric. Simply purchase a piece of fabric slightly larger than your quilt. If you are making a quilt that is twin-size or larger, you will need to piece your quilt back.

I recommend piecing your quilt back in three sections, even if the three sections are not equal in size. For a 60" × 80" (152cm × 203cm) quilt, two pieces of 45" × 60" (114cm × 152cm) fabric would be needed. Cut one piece in half parallel to the selvage, and sew each half to one side of the wide piece, creating a quilt back that is 22½"/45"/22½" (57cm/114cm/57cm). This way, when the quilt is folded, the stress of the fold will not pop open the center seam.

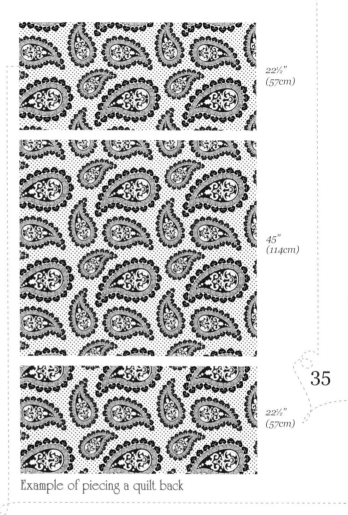

22½"
(57cm)

45"
(114cm)

22½"
(57cm)

Example of piecing a quilt back

35

3-Fabric Tip

If you prefer to use a fusible batting, place the batting sticky-side up on the pressing surface. Lay the quilt back face-up onto the batting, smoothing out any wrinkles. Following the manufacturer's instructions, gently press from the center out to the edges until the batting is fused to the backing. When you layer your quilt top face-up on the batting, you can use fewer pins to hold it in place while you do your quilting.

LAYERING AND PINNING

The quilt top, batting and backing must all be layered and pinned before the quilt stitching is done. This ensures that the layers don't move around while you sew, distorting and puckering the quilt. The quilt back and batting should each be about 2" (52cm) larger than the quilt top.

Layer your quilt in this order from bottom to top:
1. Quilt back, right-side-down
2. Batting
3. Quilt top, right-side-up

Place the quilt back right-side-down on a table or floor. Using painter's tape, tape around all four edges pulling just hard enough to eliminate any wrinkles, but not so hard that you distort the fabric.

Lay the batting on top of the backing fabric, gently smoothing out any wrinkles with your hands. The batting should be about the same size as the quilt back and should line up with the edges of the back.

Center the quilt top right-side-up on top of the batting and quilt back. Make sure there is about 1" (3cm) of batting and backing fabric showing on all four edges. Smooth the quilt top so all the seams look straight and there are no wrinkles.

Beginning in the center of the quilt, put one pin through all three layers. Set the point of the pin into the quilt until you can feel it touch the surface of the table. With a rocking motion, rock the pin up to the top again and close the pin. A Kwik Klip (see page 15) is helpful.

Continue to pin, moving in a line toward the top edge of the quilt, placing pins every 3" to 4" (8cm to 10cm). When you reach the top edge, pin from the center to the bottom, and then from the center to each side until the entire surface of the quilt is covered with pins 3" to 4" (8cm to 10cm) apart. If you have a quilting design in mind before you pin, place the pins away from the areas where you will stitch, as it is cumbersome to pull pins out as you quilt.

Tape the quilt back right-side-down to a flat surface.

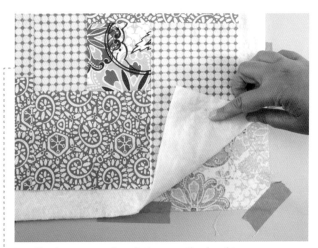

Lay the batting and quilt top on the backing.

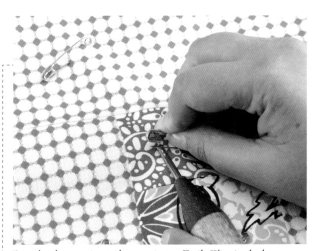

Pin the layers together, using a Kwik Klip to help.

QUILTING

The term *quilting* refers to the stitching that holds the three layers of your quilt together. Quilting can be done by hand or by machine (we will be doing ours by machine), and it can be functional or decorative. The primary purpose of quilting is to prevent the layers of the quilt from shifting during use, which can eventually cause the seams to pop open. Even a quilt that is meant to hang on a wall still needs some quilting to prevent it from stretching and sagging.

Quilting is more than functional; it is an opportunity to add another layer of complexity, making the quilt more interesting. Each of the quilts in this book has a suggested quilting design. If you wish to keep the quilting simple and functional, suggestions will be made as to where to do your functional quilting.

GET READY TO QUILT

Start by placing your walking foot on the machine. Adjust the stitch length to accommodate the thickness of the batting—this means going up one numbered increment on the stitch length setting, or even more for thicker batting.

You may find it easier, particularly with a larger quilt, to set up your machine in the lower right-hand corner of a kitchen or dining room table. This allows the portion of the quilt you are not working on to be supported flat, not pulling down. Use a chair that allows your knees to bend at a 90-degree angle to the floor, and at a height that allows your elbows to bend at a 90-degree angle to the tabletop.

THREAD

For the top of your quilt, choose a thread that is:
1. **Monofilament**: invisible thread; only the indentation of the stitching shows with no color
2. **Color**: complements or contrasts with the colors in your quilt top
3. **Variegated**: changes colors at regular intervals

For the bobbin, find a color that matches the most dominant color in the quilt back. Bobbin thread, poly, cotton or poly/cotton threads are all appropriate for the bobbin. Don't use quilting thread in a sewing machine; this thread is intended for hand quilting and will not feed properly through a machine.

STITCH-IN-THE-DITCH QUILTING

Stitch-in-the-ditch refers to quilting in a seam so that the stitches do not show. This is done when you do not wish to add any other elements to the quilt and want to simply hold the layers together.

When you sewed the quilt top together, the seam allowances were pressed to one side, so one side of each seam is slightly higher than the other (you can feel this with your finger). The area under which the seam allowance sits is called the *uphill* side of the seam; the other is the *downhill* side of the seam.

When stitching-in-the-ditch, sew on the downhill side of the seam as close to the edge of the uphill side as possible. Use the line in the center of your foot as a guide, keeping it aligned with the seam.

Stitch-in-the-ditch quilting is almost invisible on the quilt top when done with a monofilament thread in the top of the machine.

Stitch-in-the-ditch quilting

USING QUILTING TEMPLATES

There are many ways to mark a quilt for quilting—colored quilt pencils, air-erase markers, water-erase markers, chalk, stencils and all sorts of other notions. I have found that no particular method works well on all fabric colors and patterns. What might show up well on a light color doesn't work on a dark color, and some don't show up on a busy print at all. That is why I have developed my own way of quilting with a paper template.

I use a template of the design traced on either tracing paper or Golden Threads paper (see page 15). This template is pinned onto each quilt block. Stitch along the drawn lines directly through the paper, and then tear away the paper. This is the easiest way I have found to transfer the design to the quilt.

Although regular tracing paper works fine, I prefer to use Golden Threads paper. This comes in a roll that makes it easier to cut pieces for blocks larger than a sheet of tracing paper. If using tracing paper, simply tape sheets together to create a piece large enough for your quilt block.

Create several templates at once by stacking up to ten sheets. Trace the quilting design onto the top sheet. Remove the thread from your sewing machine and sew through all the layers over the drawn lines. Peel the paper layers apart. Now you will have ten identical paper templates with a dotted line to follow.

Pin one of these templates to the quilt, beginning as close to the center of the quilt as possible. The designs in this book have a registration mark on each template that ensures the template is properly placed on the block. As you did when pinning, start quilting near the center of the quilt and work out toward the edges to prevent distortion.

Trace the quilting template onto tracing or Golden Threads paper.

Stitch without thread on the drawn lines to create multiple templates.

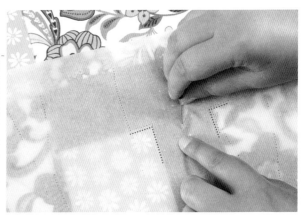

Using the registration marks, pin the templates to the quilt.

Using a walking foot, stitch on each of the template guidelines. Lock your stitches at the beginning and end of each line of stitching by holding the quilt in place for several stitches. This will prevent the stitch lines from unraveling.

After the stitching is done, carefully pull the paper off. The Golden Threads paper is very thin and will practically fall off on its own. Tracing paper may require that you score the stitch lines with a seam ripper before carefully pulling the paper out.

Continue to quilt the blocks, one at a time, working from the center toward the outside edges. When you find a quilt pin in the path of your quilting, pull it out and use straight pins to hold the template on and stabilize the block.

When all the quilting is completed, check the edges of the quilt to make sure they still appear to be straight. If they are not, make the accommodation when pinning your binding in place, using your rotary cutting ruler to measure from seams within the quilt to the edges.

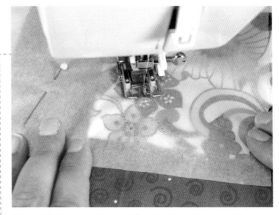

Quilt, following the perforated outline on the template.

Gently tear away the paper.

39

3-Fabric Tip

On some designs where the same line continues through many blocks, painter's tape is very helpful. Use the template to determine where the lines will go, and mark them with painter's tape instead of paper. Sew along the edge of the tape, pull it off and use the tape again to mark the next line of stitching.

BINDING

After completing all the quilt stitching, the final step in making your quilt is adding the binding to the outside edges. If you are making a wall hanging, you may want to add a rod pocket; this needs to be added before attaching the binding (see page 43).

There are several methods of binding, but I find this one to be the easiest. In this binding method, you will add binding to all four sides separately, beginning with the two long sides and then adding binding to the two short sides.

CUT AND JOIN BINDING STRIPS

Start by cutting 2½" (6cm) wide strips in the same way you cut the strips to construct your quilt. You will need enough to cover all edges. For a 40" (102cm) square quilt, you will need four strips. For a twin-sized quilt, you will need eight strips.

If your quilt side is longer than the length of a binding strip (approximately 40" [102cm]), you will need to sew two strips together with a diagonal seam. Take one strip and turn the corner of one end toward the wrong side of the fabric to make a triangle. Press this fold.

Align the end of a second strip with the folded triangle, right sides together. Carefully unfold the triangle, keeping the strips aligned, so that the strips are perpendicular to each other. Pin the strips together. Sew on the pressed line, open and trim the fabric ¼" (6mm) from the seam. For the twin-sized quilts in this book, you will need to sew two strips together for each side of the quilt using this method.

Turn the end to make a triangle.

Align another strip with the triangle.

Pin the strips together and sew on the folded line.

Cut off the excess fabric.

PREPARE THE BINDING STRIPS

If you joined binding strips, press the seam allowance open. Fold the strip in half lengthwise, right-sides-out, and press. You now have a strip with one folded edge and one raw edge. Place the raw edge along one of the raw edges of your quilt, with the folded edge laying on the quilt top. Pin in place so the pins point in the direction you will start sewing. For rectangular quilts, always begin with the longer sides.

Sew one binding strip to one quilt edge using a walking foot and ¼" (6mm) seam allowance. As when quilting, increase the stitch length slightly. Sew another binding strip to the opposite side of the quilt in the same manner. If you combined strips to make your binding longer, rotate them so that the diagonal seams in the binding are at opposite ends of the quilt. This will make the binding seams less obvious than if they line up from side to side.

Trim the batting and backing fabric so that it extends about ½" (13mm) from the seam line (or ¼" [6mm] from the edge of the quilt top). Roll the binding over the edge to the back, and position the folded edge of the binding so that it covers the stitches. Trim and pin in place at the beginning and end of each binding strip.

(continued on page 42)

Press the seam allowance open.

Press the binding strip in half.

41

Align the raw edges of the binding and the quilt.

Sew the binding strip to the quilt edge.

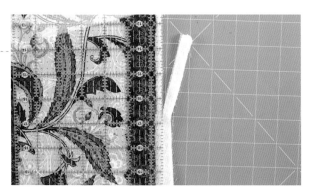

Trim excess batting ¼" (6mm) from quilt top edge.

Roll the binding over the quilt to the back and pin.

(continued from page 41)

The bindings that go across the remaining two sides of the quilt are done in the same way, but with one extra step: To achieve a clean corner, fold under the end of the strip ½" (13mm) and refold the binding strip in half.

Line up the folded end of the strip with the edge of the existing binding so that it sits right at the very edge. Pin and sew until you are a few inches from the other end. Stop sewing and fold this end under, trimming as needed, so that it also ends right at the edge of the perpendicular binding. When you roll this binding edge to the back, the corner will look neat and square. Do the same on the last remaining side of the quilt.

The binding strips must now be sewn down on the back. This can be done by machine or by hand. Personally, I like finishing by hand; I think it looks nicer and I enjoy having a little hand sewing to do while watching TV with my family. Sewing binding by machine is faster. The choice is yours.

FINISHING THE BINDING BY MACHINE

To finish the binding by machine, roll the binding strips to the back, and pin in place so that the folded edge covers the line of stitching. From the front, insert pins so that the tips of the pins point to your starting place. Flip the quilt over and make sure that every pin has caught the folded edge of the binding on the back, and that the binding all looks evenly spaced. Now is the time to make any adjustments. Using invisible thread on top and bobbin thread that matches the binding, stitch-in-the-ditch from the quilt top with a walking foot. Pull the pins out as you reach them.

42

Turn under the binding end ½" (13mm), and fold back in half.

Align the folded edge with the edge of the existing binding, pin and sew in place.

Roll the binding to the back and pin in place.

Stitch in the ditch from the top of the quilt.

SEWING THE BINDING BY HAND

To sew the binding in place by hand, I recommend using a hand appliqué stitch. Choose a thread that matches the binding. Monofilament thread is very difficult to work with by hand, so use a cotton, poly or poly/cotton thread for hand sewing.

Thread your needle, double the thread and knot the end. You do not want the thread to be longer than the length from your hand to your elbow. You will have fewer tangles in the thread if you thread the needle in the same direction the thread comes off the spool.

First, put the needle into the quilt back under the binding strip, and pull the needle up in the fold. Now put the needle into the quilt backing next to where it came out of the fold, and go into the batting, being careful to not stitch through the front of the quilt. Travel sideways about ¼" (6mm) and come up again through the fold of the binding. When you pull the thread through, only a tiny dot of thread will show at the edge of the binding. Continue to travel along, taking a stitch about every ¼" (6mm). Be careful not to stitch through the quilt top. Repeat all along the binding strips.

Pull the needle up in the binding fold.

Travel sideways and come up again in the fold.

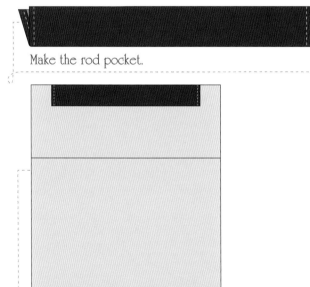

Make the rod pocket.

Align the pocket with the top of the quilt back.

OPTIONAL: HANGING ROD POCKET

If you plan to hang your quilt, you will want to add a pocket to the back through which a hanging rod can be placed. Keep in mind that this pocket should be added *before* sewing on the quilt binding.

1. Cut a piece of fabric 8½" (22cm) long and 2" (5cm) narrower than the width of your quilt.
2. Press the two short edges under approximately ¼" (6mm).
3. Turn the same edges under a second time and press in place.
4. Stitch the turned-under edges in place.
5. Fold the piece of fabric in half lengthwise.
6. Carefully center the rod pocket on the top edge of the back of the quilt, aligning the raw edges of the rod pocket with the top raw edge of the back.
7. Sew binding on as usual: Roll the binding to the back of the quilt and stitch in place by machine or hand, catching the rod pocket inside.
8. Slip stitch the bottom of the rod pocket to the quilt back.

OOPS! Fixing Common Mistakes

I HAVE TO RIP OUT AND START AGAIN

It happens to all of us at some time or another—we sew something wrong-side-up, sew the wrong edge or simply sew the wrong pieces together. At some point, you will need to tear out a seam to fix a mistake.

The seam ripper is an inexpensive and invaluable tool to have in your sewing box. Slide the point of the seam ripper under a stitch and up, breaking the thread. The fastest and easiest way to pull out a seam is to break a stitch every five or ten stitches, then gently pull on the fabrics and the whole thing should pull apart. Don't tug too hard or you could rip the fabric. Cut through any resistant spots of thread with the seam ripper.

Break a stitch every five or ten stitches.

MY BLOCKS ARE NOT THE SAME SIZE AS THOSE IN THE INSTRUCTIONS

There are a lot of reasons your blocks may not be exactly the same size as those in the instructions; perhaps you cut your strips slightly larger or smaller than mine, or sewed with a slightly smaller or larger seam allowance.

What is more important is that your blocks are the same size as each other. It may mean your quilt isn't exactly the same size as mine, but it still will go together without a problem—and who will ever know?

THE BLOCKS ARE DIFFERENT SIZES

Sometimes you will find that one or two of your blocks are not the same size as the others. This happens, and it doesn't mean the blocks can't be used, nor does it mean that you should cut all the other blocks smaller to match.

Once you determine which blocks are smaller, mark them with a pin or sticky note. If the block is less than ½" (13mm) smaller than the others, center the smaller block on the adjacent larger block and use the larger block as the guide when sewing your ¼" (6mm) seam allowance. The shortage will be absorbed into the seam allowance. If the seam allowance comes very close to the edge of the smaller block, go over the stitches a second time to insure they won't pop out.

If your block is more than ½" (13mm) off, you can slightly stretch the size of a smaller block by blocking it, described in *The Blocks Are Not Straight* (see page 45).

ONE PART OF THE BLOCK IS SHORTER THAN OTHERS

As in the case of the smaller block, don't trim down to the shorter area if the rest of the block is the right size. Let the shortage be absorbed into the seam allowance and no one will ever know!

THE BLOCKS ARE NOT STRAIGHT

When your block doesn't look straight, you have two choices. First, if it is large enough to trim down, line up the seams in the block with your ruler and trim the block to the proper size. If there is not enough extra to trim the block, you can *block* it.

Blocking is similar to what you do when you wash a sweater—you coax the quilt block into shape. Start by placing your block on your ironing surface. Use a spray bottle to mist the block so that it is damp, not soaking wet. When fabric is moist, it has more stretch than it would have when dry, so now you can gently pull the block into position and pin on all four sides. Adjust the block so that the seams line up with your ruler. Lines on your ironing board cover can help in this process. Pin all around the edges of the block, sticking the pins straight down into the ironing board, pulling gently and misting again if necessary. Then leave the block to dry or press it with a steam iron.

This method can also slightly increase the size of a block that is a bit too small.

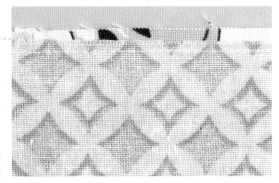

Absorb the shortage in the seam allowance.

Block an uneven square with water.

45

WHEN SEWING ROWS TOGETHER, SOME BLOCKS DON'T LINE UP AT THE SEAM EDGES

If you didn't notice earlier that some of your blocks are not the same size as the others, you may notice it now that you are trying to line up the row intersections. Fabric has a fair amount of stretch in it, so line up the seam intersections with a pin (see page 34). The larger block will have some puckering. With the smaller block on top, pull gently on the smaller block as it goes through the sewing machine so that the pinned intersections match as the blocks are sewn together. Press as sewn first (see page 30), allowing the fabric to relax into the sewn position.

3-Fabric Tip

Having trouble pinning the binding for machine stitching? Use a small amount of fabric glue or basting glue to hold the binding in place while you sew. Put a very thin line of glue just above the stitch line on the quilt back. Roll the binding into place and press with a warm iron to set the glue. Now you can attach the binding by stitching in the ditch from the front without any pins. Make sure that the binding comes down far enough on the back to be caught in the stitching.

The projects in this section are divided into three categories, arranged in order according to difficulty. Follow the instructions to complete the quilt top, and refer to chapter one for help with finishing and binding. Every project includes yardage and instructions for both a small and a twin-sized quilt.

2 THE PROJECTS

1 ONE-BLOCK QUILTS
Just one block makes up each of the quilts in this section. Arrange the blocks symmetrically or randomly for different looks.

2 TWO-BLOCK QUILTS
Make two different blocks and move them around for lots of interesting combinations and arrangements. Think all blocks need to be square? Think again! More possibilities equals more fun.

3 STRIP-SET QUILTS
These quilts are so quick and easy you don't even need to make blocks. Sew strips together and rearrange them into great-looking quilts.

47

Simplici-T

This simple block goes together in just two steps, making for a quick-and-easy starter project. It's great as a first quilt or a weekend project.

CHOOSING FABRICS:

- Fabric 1: accent fabric (yellow print in sample)

- Fabric 2: lighter value (white and black daisy print in sample)

- Fabric 3: darker value (black with white stripe in sample)

- Backing fabric

- Binding fabric: complementary fabric of your choice

• All strips are cut the width of the fabric (WOF), approximately 42" to 45" (107cm to 114cm).
• Fabric used for the quilt back must measure at least 43" (109cm) wide.

SMALL QUILT (SHOWN)
Finished Block: 10" × 10" (25cm × 25cm)
Finished Quilt: 40" × 40" (102cm × 102cm)

FABRIC	YARDAGE	CUTS	FOR
Fabric 1	1 yd. (91cm)	• (10) 2½" (6cm) strips	Strip Set
Fabric 2	1 yd. (91cm)	• (4) 5½" (14cm) strips	Strip Set
Fabric 3	½ yd. (46cm)	• (4) 3½" (9cm) strips	Strip Set
Quilt Back	1¼ yds. (1.1m)	(refer to page 35)	Quilt Back
Binding	½ yd. (46cm)	(refer to page 40)	Quilt Binding

TWIN QUILT
Finished Block: 10" × 10" (25cm × 25cm)
Finished Quilt: 60" × 80" (152cm × 203cm)

FABRIC	YARDAGE	CUTS	FOR
Fabric 1	2¼ yds. (2m)	• (28) 2½" (6cm) strips	Strip Set
Fabric 2	2 yds. (1.8m)	• (12) 5½" (14cm) strips	Strip Set
Fabric 3	1½ yds. (1.4m)	• (12) 3½" (9cm) strips	Strip Set
Quilt Back	4 yds. (3.7m)	(refer to page 35)	Quilt Back
Binding	¾ yd. (23cm)	(refer to page 40)	Quilt Binding

CONSTRUCT THE BLOCK

1 Make the strip set. Sew strips together in this order: a 3½" strip of Fabric 3, a 2½" strip of Fabric 1 and a 5½" strip of Fabric 2. The resulting strip set is light/accent/dark. Press seam allowances in one direction. Make four strip sets for the small quilt or twelve for the twin quilt.

2 Cut the strip set into sections every 8½" (22cm). (This is easily done with a large square ruler, a combination of two rulers or by using the grid on your cutting mat.) This is Unit A. Make sixteen A units for the small quilt or forty-eight for the twin quilt.

Fabric 3

Fabric 1

Fabric 2

Make Strip Set

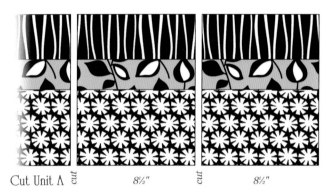

Cut Unit A — *cut* — 8½" — *cut* — 8½"

3 Place a 2½" strip of Fabric 1 right-side-up in the sewing machine. Place an A unit right-side-down on the strip so that the Fabric 3 piece is at the top. With the right-hand raw edges aligned, sew the unit to the strip. Sew all the Unit A pieces to the Fabric 1 strips in this way.

flip

Fabric 3

Fabric 1 strip

Unit A

Sew Units to Strip

press

Complete the Block

4 Press seam allowances toward the Fabric 1 strip. Cut the sections apart at the edges of the units, lining up the perpendicular seams with your ruler. Press. This completes your block. Each block should measure 10½" × 10½" (27cm × 27cm). Make sixteen blocks for the small quilt or forty-eight for the twin quilt.

3-Fabric Tip

Once you have sewn your block, line up the ruler so that the seam lines are straight, both horizontally and vertically. If the edges of the block are not straight, adjustments can be made when sewing them to another block, but the seams are now a permanent part of your quilt, so make sure they look straight in the ruler.

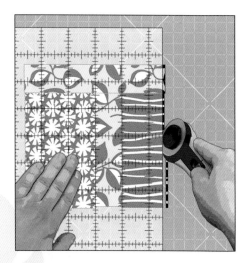

Modern Basket Weave

Basket-weave designs are classic in quilting, but this one is different because the seam lines don't need to be lined up when the blocks are connected. For this quilt, a random arrangement of blocks is not recommended—only by alternating the blocks will you achieve the basket-weave effect.

CHOOSING FABRICS:

- Fabric 1: lightest value (light blue circle print in sample)

- Fabric 2: medium value (medium blue in sample)

- Fabric 3: darkest value or accent color (green leaf print in sample)

- Backing fabric

- Binding fabric: complementary fabric of your choice

54

• All strips are cut the width of the fabric (WOF), approximately 42" to 45" (107cm to 114cm).
• Fabric used for the quilt back must measure at least 43" (109cm) wide.
• Depending on the true width of the fabric, you may need to cut additional strips. The yardage for any additional strips is built into the yardage requirements below.

SMALL QUILT
Finished Block: 12" × 12" (30cm × 30cm)
Finished Quilt: 36" × 36" (91cm × 91cm)

FABRIC	YARDAGE	CUTS	FOR
Fabric 1	¾ yd. (69cm)	• (1) 3½" (9cm) strip	Strip Set A
		• (1) 5½" (14cm) strip	Strip Set A
		• (2) 2½" (6cm) strips	Strip Set B
Fabric 2	¾ yd. (69cm)	• (1) 4½" (11cm) strip	Strip Set A
		• (1) 8½" (22cm) strip	Strip Set B
Fabric 3	½ yd. (46cm)	• (3) 4½" (11cm) strips	Center Strip
Quilt Back	1¼ yds. (1.1m)	(refer to page 35)	Quilt Back
Binding	½ yd. (46cm)	(refer to page 40)	Quilt Binding

TWIN QUILT (SHOWN)
Finished Block: 12" × 12" (30cm × 30cm)
Finished Quilt: 60" × 84" (152cm × 213cm)

FABRIC	YARDAGE	CUTS	FOR
Fabric 1	2 yds. (1.8m)	• (4) 3½" (9cm) strips	Strip Set A
		• (4) 5½" (14cm) strips	Strip Set A
		• (8) 2½" (6cm) strips	Strip Set B
Fabric 2	2 yds. (1.8m)	• (4) 4½" (11cm) strips	Strip Set A
		• (4) 8½" (22cm) strips	Strip Set B
Fabric 3	1¾ yds. (1.6m)	• (12) 4½" (11cm) strips	Center Strip
Quilt Back	4 yds. (3.7m)	(refer to page 35)	Quilt Back
Binding	¾ yd. (69cm)	(refer to page 40)	Quilt Binding

For metric measurements, refer to the charts on page 55.

CONSTRUCT THE BLOCK

1 Make Strip Set A. Sew strips together in this order: a 3½" strip of Fabric 1, a 4½" strip of Fabric 2 and a 5½" strip of Fabric 1. Press seam allowances toward the 5½" strip. Make one strip set for the small quilt or four for the twin quilt.

2 Cut the strip set into sections every 4½" (11cm). This is Unit A. Make nine A units for the small quilt or thirty-five for the twin quilt.

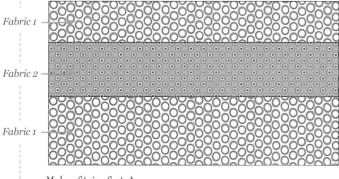

Fabric 1
Fabric 2
Fabric 1

Make Strip Set A

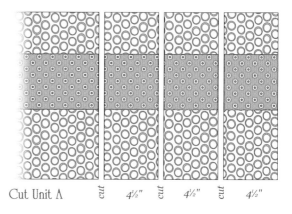

Cut Unit A   *cut*   4½"   *cut*   4½"   *cut*   4½"

56

3 Make Strip Set B. Sew strips together in this order: a 2½" strip of Fabric 1, an 8½" strip of Fabric 2 and a 2½" strip of Fabric 1. Press seam allowances in one direction. Make one strip set for the small quilt or four for the twin quilt.

4 Cut the strip set into sections every 4½" (11cm). This is Unit B. Make nine B units for the small quilt or thirty-five for the twin quilt.

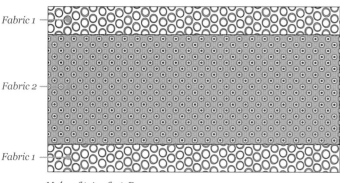

Fabric 1
Fabric 2
Fabric 1

Make Strip Set B

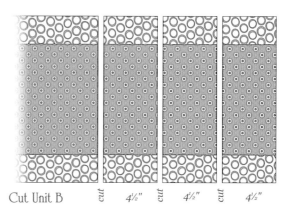

Cut Unit B   *cut*   4½"   *cut*   4½"   *cut*   4½"

5 Place a 4½"
center strip of
Fabric 3 right-
side-up in the sewing
machine. Place an A
unit right-side-down
on top of the strip
so that the narrow
Fabric 1 piece is at
the top. With the
right-hand raw edges
aligned, sew the unit
to the strip. Sew all
the Unit A pieces to
the Fabric 3 strips
this way.

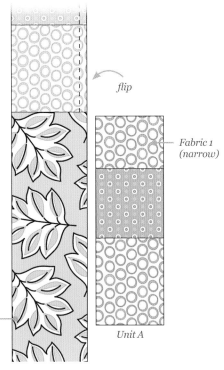

flip

Fabric 1 (narrow)

Fabric 3 strip

Unit A

Sew Units to Strip

6 Press seam
allowances
toward the Fabric
3 center strip. Cut the
sections apart at the
edges of the units.

press

Complete the Partial Block

57

7 Chain piece the B units to the
other side of the Fabric 3 center
strip of each partial block. This
completes your block. Press. Each block
should measure 12½" × 12½" (32cm ×
32cm). Make nine blocks for the small
quilt or thirty-five for the twin quilt.

Fabric 3 strip

Unit B   *Unit A*

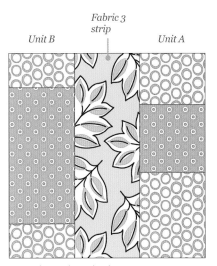

Complete the Block

ASSEMBLE AND FINISH THE QUILT

1 Arrange the blocks into rows, alternately orienting the center strip horizontally and vertically to create the basket-weave effect. The first block of each row should alternate horizontally or vertically, as shown. For the small quilt, make **three rows of three blocks** each. For the twin quilt, make **seven rows of five blocks** each.

2 Sew the blocks into rows. Press the seam allowances of the odd-numbered rows to the right and the seam allowances of the even-numbered rows to the left. Sew the rows together to complete the quilt top.

3 Carefully press and square off the quilt top, and prepare the backing and batting. Layer and pin the quilt, referring to page 36.

4 For functional quilting, stitch-in-the-ditch around each block and at the edges of the center strip to emphasize the basket-weave pattern. Use the template provided on page 121 for more decorative quilting.

5 Bind the quilt to finish.

58

Small Quilt Layout

Template Quilting Pattern

Twin Quilt Layout

Around the Corner

This block, completed in three simple steps, looks far more complex than it is. The right angle in the design creates lots of visual excitement and movement. Remember to vary the values of your your small-, medium- and large-scale prints.

CHOOSING FABRICS:

• Fabric 1: largest-scale print (rose print in sample)

• Fabric 2: medium-scale print (yellow print in sample)

• Fabric 3: smallest-scale print (green print in sample)

• Backing fabric

• Binding fabric: complementary fabric of your choice

• All strips are cut the width of the fabric (WOF), approximately 42" to 45" (107cm to 114cm).
• Fabric used for the quilt back must measure at least 43" (109cm) wide.

SMALL QUILT (SHOWN)
Finished Block: 10" × 10" (25cm × 25cm)
Finished Quilt: 36" × 36" (91cm × 91cm)

FABRIC	YARDAGE	CUTS	FOR
Fabric 1	1 yd. (91cm)	• (3) 6½" (17cm) strips • (1) 7" (18cm) strip	Strip Set A Strip Set C
Fabric 2	¾ yd. (69cm)	• (3) 4½" (11cm) strips • (1) 3" (8cm) strip • (3) 2" (5cm) strips	Strip Set A Strip Set B Center Strip
Fabric 3	½ yd. (46cm)	• (1) 8" (20cm) strip • (1) 6" (15cm) strip	Strip Set B Strip Set C
Quilt Back	1¼ yds. (1.1m)	(refer to page 35)	Quilt Back
Binding	½ yd. (46cm)	(refer to page 40)	Quilt Binding

TWIN QUILT
Finished Block: 10" × 10" (25cm × 25cm)
Finished Quilt: 60" × 84" (152cm × 213cm)

FABRIC	YARDAGE	CUTS	FOR
Fabric 1	2½ yds. (2.3m)	• (9) 6½" (17cm) strips • (3) 7" (18cm) strip	Strip Set A Strip Set C
Fabric 2	2¼ yds. (2m)	• (9) 4½" (11cm) strips • (3) 3" (8cm) strip • (12) 2" (5cm) strips	Strip Set A Strip Set B Center Strip
Fabric 3	1¼ yds. (1.1m)	• (3) 8" (20cm) strip • (3) 6" (15cm) strip	Strip Set B Strip Set C
Quilt Back	4 yds. (3.7m)	(refer to page 35)	Quilt Back
Binding	¾ yd. (69cm)	(refer to page 40)	Quilt Binding

For metric measurements, refer to the charts on page 61.

CONSTRUCT THE BLOCK

1 Make Strip Set A. Sew together one 4½" strip of Fabric 2 and one 6½" strip of Fabric 1. Press seam allowances toward Fabric 1. Cut the strip set into sections every 8½" (22cm). (This is easily done with a large square ruler, a combination of two rulers or by using the grid on your cutting mat.) This is Unit A. Make nine A units for the small quilt or thirty-five for the twin quilt.

2 Make Strip Set B. Sew together one 3" strip of Fabric 2 and one 8" strip of Fabric 3. Press seam allowances toward Fabric 3. Cut the strip set into sections every 3" (8cm). This is Unit 1B. Make nine 1B units for the small quilt or thirty-five for the twin quilt.

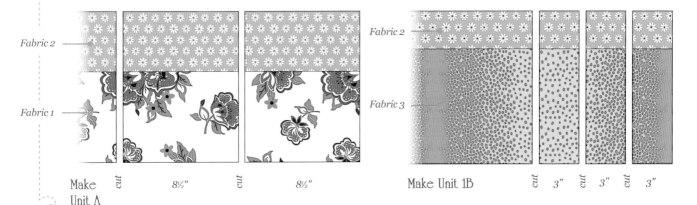

Fabric 2

Fabric 1

Make Unit A   *cut*   8½"   *cut*   8½"

Fabric 2

Fabric 3

Make Unit 1B   *cut* 3" *cut* 3" *cut* 3"

62

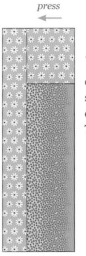

flip

3 Place a 2" center strip of Fabric 2 right-side-up in the sewing machine. Place a 1B unit right-side-down on top of the strip so that the Fabric 3 piece is at the bottom. With the right-hand raw edges aligned, sew the unit to the strip. Sew all the Unit 1B pieces to the Fabric 2 center strips this way.

Fabric 2 strip

Fabric 3

Unit 1B

Sew Units to Strip

press

4 Press seam allowances toward the center strip. Cut the sections apart at the edges of the units. This is now Unit B.

Complete Unit B

5 Sew each Unit A to a Unit B, referring to the image below for layout arrangement. Make sure that the long Fabric 2 strip is in the center when the units are combined. Chain piece all units together in this way, cut apart and press seam allowances toward the center strip.

6 Make Strip Set C. Sew one 6" strip of Fabric 3 to one 7" strip of Fabric 1. Press seam allowances in one direction. Cut the strip set into sections every 2½" (6cm). This is Unit C. Make nine C units for the small quilt or thirty-five for the twin quilt.

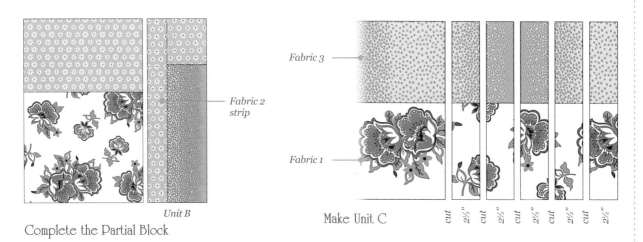

Unit B

Fabric 2 strip

Complete the Partial Block

Fabric 3

Fabric 1

Make Unit C

cut 2½" cut 2½" cut 2½" cut 2½" cut 2½"

7 Sew one Unit C to each partial block referring to the image for layout arrangement. Make sure that the Fabric 3 section of Unit C connects with Unit A of the partial block.

8 Chain piece all units to complete the blocks. Cut apart the blocks and press. Each block should measure 12½" × 12½" (32cm × 32cm). Make nine blocks for the small quilt or thirty-five for the twin quilt.

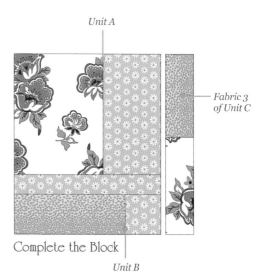

Unit A

Fabric 3 of Unit C

Complete the Block

Unit B

63

ASSEMBLE AND FINISH THE QUILT

1 Arrange the blocks in any design that you like, either symmetrically or randomly. It may help to lay them out on a bed or on the floor.

2 For the small quilt, sew the blocks into **three rows of three blocks**. For the twin quilt, sew the blocks into **seven rows of five blocks**. Press seam allowances of even-numbered rows in one direction; press seam allowances of odd-numbered rows in the opposite direction. Sew the rows together to complete the quilt top.

3 Carefully press and square off the quilt top, and prepare the backing and batting. Layer and pin the quilt, referring to page 36.

4 For functional quilting, stitch-in-the-ditch. Use the template provided on page 121 for more decorative quilting.

5 Bind the quilt to finish.

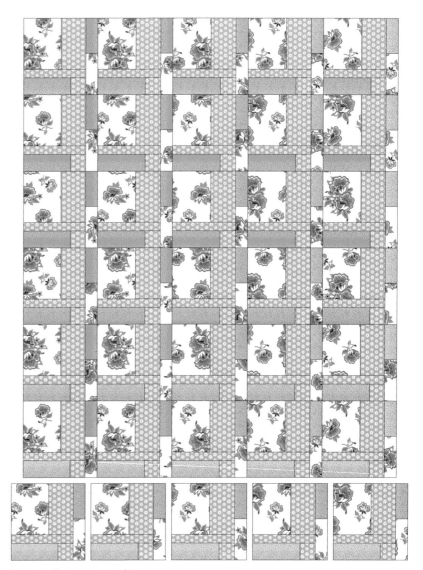

Twin Quilt Symmetrical Layout

Template Quilting Pattern

Small Quilt Random Layout

Dancing Squares

This quilt is made from one block constructed in two units. The little squares in the blocks seem to dance around the surface of the quilt. Arranged either symmetrically or randomly, this quilt looks more complex than it actually is.

CHOOSING FABRICS:

- Fabric 1: medium value or accent color, smallest-scale print (medium blue in sample)

- Fabric 2: lightest value, largest-scale print (paisley print in sample)

- Fabric 3: darkest value, medium-scale print (dark blue swirl print in sample)

- Backing fabric

- Binding fabric: complementary fabric of your choice

• All strips are cut the width of the fabric (WOF), approximately 42" to 45" (107cm to 114cm).
• Fabric used for the quilt back must measure at least 42" (107cm) wide.

SMALL QUILT (SHOWN)
Finished Block: 10" × 10" (25cm × 25cm)
Finished Quilt: 40" × 40" (102cm × 102cm)

FABRIC	YARDAGE	CUTS	FOR
Fabric 1	½ yd. (46cm)	• (2) 3½" (9cm) strips	Unit B
Fabric 2	1 yd. (91cm)	• (2) 8½" (22cm) strips	Unit A
		• (3) 3" (8cm) strips	Unit B
Fabric 3	1 yd. (91cm)	• (4) 2½" (6cm) strips	Units A and B
		• (3) 5½" (14cm) strips	Unit B
Quilt Back	1¼ yds. (1.1m)	(refer to page 35)	Quilt Back
Binding	½ yd. (46cm)	(refer to page 40)	Quilt Binding

TWIN QUILT
Finished Block: 10" × 10" (25cm × 25cm)
Finished Quilt: 60" × 80" (152cm × 203cm)

FABRIC	YARDAGE	CUTS	FOR
Fabric 1	¾ yd. (69cm)	• (5) 3½" (9cm) strips	Unit B
Fabric 2	2¼ yds. (2m)	• (6) 8½" (22cm) strips	Unit A
		• (7) 3" (8cm) strips	Unit B
Fabric 3	2¼ yds. (2m)	• (11) 2½" (6cm) strips	Units A and B
		• (7) 5½" (14cm) strips	Unit B
Quilt Back	4 yds. (3.7m)	(refer to page 35)	Quilt Back
Binding	¾ yd. (69cm)	(refer to page 40)	Quilt Binding

For metric measurements, refer to the charts on page 67.

CONSTRUCT THE BLOCK

1 Make the first strip set. Sew together a 2½" strip of Fabric 3 and an 8½" strip of Fabric 2. Press seam allowances toward Fabric 3. Make two strip sets for the small quilt or six for the twin quilt. Cut the strip set into sections every 5" (13cm). This is Unit A. Make sixteen A units for the small quilt or forty-eight for the twin quilt.

2 Make the second strip set. Sew together a 2½" strip of Fabric 3 and a 3½" strip of Fabric 1. Press seam allowances toward Fabric 1. Make two strip sets for the small quilt or five for the twin quilt. Cut the strip set into sections every 3½" (9cm). This is Unit 1B. Make sixteen 1B units for the small quilt or forty-eight for the twin quilt.

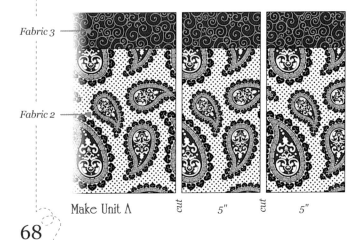

Fabric 3

Fabric 2

Make Unit A   *cut*   5"   *cut*   5"

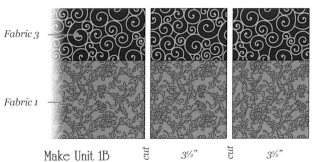

Fabric 3

Fabric 1

Make Unit 1B   *cut*   3½"   *cut*   3½"

68

3 Place a 3" strip of Fabric 2 right-side-up in the sewing machine. Place a 1B unit right-side-down on the strip so that the Fabric 3 piece is at the top. With the right-hand raw edges aligned, sew the unit to the strip. Sew all of the Unit 1B pieces to the 3" Fabric 2 strips in this way.

flip

Fabric 2 strip

Fabric 3

Unit 1B

Sew Units to Strip

press

Complete Unit 2B

4 Press seam allowance toward the Fabric 2 strip. Cut the sections apart at the edges of the units, lining up the seams with your ruler. This is now Unit 2B.

Fabric
3 strip

Sew Units to Strip

5 Place a 5½" strip of Fabric 3 right-side-up in the sewing machine. Place a 2B unit right-side-down on the strip, making sure raw edges align on the right-hand side, so that the Fabric 2 piece is at the top and the Fabric 1 piece is directly underneath. Sew all the Unit 2B pieces to the 5½" Fabric 3 strips.

flip

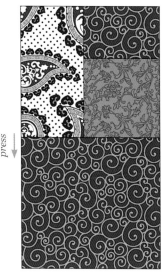

Fabric 2

Unit 2B

6 Press seam allowances toward the Fabric 3 strip. Cut the sections apart at the edges of the units, lining up the seams with your ruler. This is now the completed Unit B.

press

Complete Unit B

7 Next to your sewing machine, make one pile of the A units, all oriented with Fabric 3 at the top. Next to them, make a pile of the B units, all oriented with Fabric 2 at the top. Flip one Unit A onto one Unit B with right sides together and aligned along the right edges.

8 Pin the intersection of the first seam on each unit to ensure that the seams line up and the block goes together in the right order, or lock the seams together with your fingers (see page 34). Chain piece all the blocks. Press. Each block should measure 10½" × 10½" (27cm × 27cm). Make sixteen blocks for the small quilt or forty-eight for the twin quilt.

Fabric 2   Fabric 3

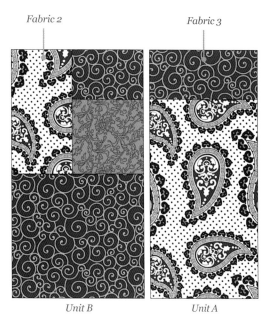

Unit B   Unit A

Sew Unit A to Unit B

69

ASSEMBLE AND
FINISH THE QUILT

1 Arrange the blocks in any design that you like, either symmetrically or randomly. It may help to lay them out on a bed or on the floor.

2 For the small quilt, sew the blocks into **four rows of four blocks**. For the twin quilt, sew the blocks into **eight rows of six blocks**. Press seam allowances of even-numbered rows in one direction; press seam allowances of odd-numbered rows in the opposite direction. Sew the rows together to complete the quilt top.

3 Carefully press and square off the quilt top, and prepare the backing and batting. Layer and pin the quilt, referring to page 36.

4 When using functional or decorative quilting, begin by stitching-in-the-ditch around the edges of all the blocks. For functional quilting, finish by stitching-in-the-ditch around the small squares of each block. Use the circular templates provided on page 121 for decorative quilting.

5 Bind the quilt to finish.

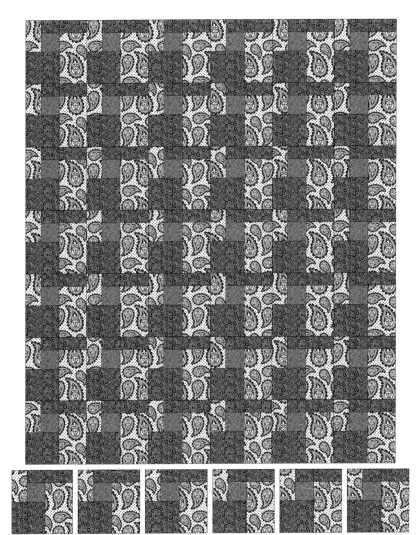

Twin Quilt Symmetrical Layout

Template Quilting Pattern

Small Quilt Random Layout

City Windows

Inspired by the windows of apartment buildings, this quilt is made up of two different rectangular blocks. Arrange the blocks symmetrically or asymmetrically to create a variety of different designs.

CHOOSING FABRICS:

- Fabric 1: lightest value, largest-scale print (multicolored floral in sample)

- Fabric 2: medium value, medium-scale print (aqua with leaf in sample)

- Fabric 3: darkest value, smallest-scale print (violet tone-on-tone in sample)

- Backing fabric

- Binding fabric: complementary fabric of your choice

• All strips are cut the width of the fabric (WOF), approximately 42" to 45" (107cm to 114cm).
• Fabric used for the quilt back must measure at least 43" (109cm) wide.

SMALL QUILT (SHOWN)
Finished Blocks: 12" × 8" (30cm × 20cm)
Finished Quilt: 36" × 40" (91cm × 102cm)

FABRIC	YARDAGE	CUTS	FOR
Fabric 1	¾ yd. (69cm)	• (2) 3½" (9cm) strips	Block A
		• (2) 6½" (17cm) strips	Block B
Fabric 2	1 yd. (91cm)	• (2) 5½" (14cm) strips	Block A
		• (2) 3½" (9cm) strips	Block A
		• (2) 4½" (11cm) strips	Block B
Fabric 3	½ yd. (46cm)	• (2) 2½" (6cm) strips	Block A
		• (2) 2½" (6cm) strips	Block B
Quilt Back	1¼ yds. (1.1m)	(refer to page 35)	Quilt Back
Binding	½ yd. (46cm)	(refer to page 40)	Quilt Binding

TWIN QUILT
Finished Blocks: 12" × 8" (30cm × 20cm)
Finished Quilt: 64" × 84" (163cm × 213cm)

FABRIC	YARDAGE	CUTS	FOR
Fabric 1	2 yds. (1.8m)	• (6) 3½" (9cm) strips	Block A
		• (7) 6½" (17cm) strips	Block B
Fabric 2	2¾ yds. (2.5m)	• (6) 5½" (14cm) strips	Block A
		• (7) 3½" (9cm) strips	Block A
		• (7) 4½" (11cm) strips	Block B
Fabric 3	1¼ yds. (1.1m)	• (7) 2½" (6cm) strips	Block A
		• (7) 2½" (6cm) strips	Block B
Quilt Back	4 yds. (3.7m)	(refer to page 35)	Quilt Back
Binding	¾ yd. (69cm)	(refer to page 40)	Quilt Binding

For metric measurements, refer to the charts on page 73.

CONSTRUCT THE A BLOCK

1 Make the first strip set. Sew a 5½" strip of Fabric 2 to a 3½" strip of Fabric 1. Press seam allowances toward Fabric 1. Make two strip sets for the small quilt or six strip sets for the twin quilt.

2 Cut the strip sets into sections every 7½" (19cm). (This is easily done with a large square ruler, a combination of two rulers or by using the grid on your cutting mat.) This is Unit 1A. Make ten 1A units for the small quilt or thirty for the twin quilt.

Fabric 2

Fabric 1

Make Strip Set

Cut
Unit 1A   *cut*   7½"   *cut*   7½"

3 Make the second strip set. Sew a 2½" strip of Fabric 3 to a 3½" strip of Fabric 2. Press seam allowances toward Fabric 3. Make two strip sets for the small quilt or seven for the twin quilt.

4 Place this strip right-side-up in the sewing machine with the Fabric 3 strip on the right. Place Unit 1A right-side-down on this strip set so that the Fabric 2 piece is at the top. With the right-hand raw edges aligned, sew the unit to the strip. Sew all the Unit 1A pieces to the strip sets in this way.

Fabric 3

Fabric 2

Make Strip Set

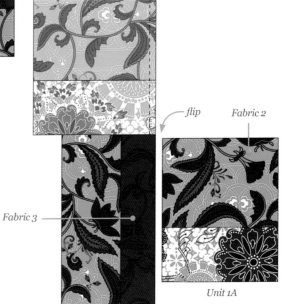

flip   *Fabric 2*

Fabric 3

Unit 1A

Sew Units to Strip Set

Complete Block A

5 Press the seam allowances toward the Fabric 3 strip. Cut the sections apart at the edges of the units, lining up the seams with your ruler. This is now Block A. Press. Each block should measure 8½" × 12½" (22cm × 32cm). Make ten A blocks for the small quilt or thirty for the twin quilt.

CONSTRUCT THE B BLOCK

1 Make the strip set. Sew strips together in this order: a 6½" strip of Fabric 1, a 4½" strip of Fabric 2 and a 2½" strip of Fabric 3. Press seam allowances in one direction. Make two strip sets for the small quilt or seven strip sets for the twin quilt.

2 Cut the strip sets into sections every 8½" (22cm). (This is easily down with a large square ruler, a combination of two rulers, or by using the grid on your cutting mat.) This is Block B. Press. Each block should measure 8½" × 12½" (22cm × 32cm). Make eight B blocks for the small quilt or twenty-eight for the twin quilt.

Fabric 1
Fabric 2
Fabric 3

Make Strip Set

Cut
Block B

cut   8½"   *cut*   8½"

ASSEMBLE AND FINISH THE QUILT

1 For the small quilt, you will need fifteen blocks to complete the quilt top. For the twin quilt, you will need fifty-six total blocks. (You will have a few extra blocks.) Arrange the blocks in any design that you like, either symmetrically or randomly. It may help to lay them out on a bed or on the floor.

2 For the small quilt, sew the blocks into **three rows of five blocks**. For the twin quilt, sew the blocks into **eight rows of seven blocks**. Press seam allowances of even-numbered rows in one direction; press seam allowances of odd-numbered rows in the opposite direction. Sew the rows together to complete the quilt top.

3 Carefully press and square off the quilt top, and prepare the backing and batting. Layer and pin the quilt, referring to page 36.

4 For functional quilting, stitch-in-the-ditch around each block and at the edges of Fabric 1. Use the template provided on page 122 for more decorative quilting.

5 Bind the quilt to finish.

76

Twin Quilt Symmetrical Layout

Block A Template Quilting Pattern

Block B Template Quilting Pattern

Small Quilt Random Layout

Fun With Stripes

I love using striped fabric in my quilts. The stripe can bring together many of the colors from other fabrics. This quilt can certainly be made without a striped fabric, but using the stripe in the blocks and the binding makes the quilt more exciting. The stripe in the pictured quilt is printed parallel to the selvage. If you choose a stripe that is printed perpendicular to the selvage, your blocks will look a little different.

CHOOSING FABRICS:

- Fabric 1: accent color (green in sample)
- Fabric 2: stripe
- Fabric 3: largest-scale print (blue creature print in sample)
- Backing fabric
- Binding fabric: striped fabric, or complementary fabric of your choice

• All strips are cut the width of the fabric (WOF), approximately 42" to 45" (107cm to 114cm).
• Fabric used for the quilt back must measure at least 43" (109cm) wide.

SMALL QUILT
Finished Blocks: 12" × 12" (30cm × 30cm)
Finished Quilt: 36" × 36" (91cm × 91cm)

FABRIC	YARDAGE	CUTS	FOR
Fabric 1	½ yd. (46cm)	• (1) 5" (13cm) strip	Block A
		• (1) 5½" (14cm) strip	Block A
		• (2) 2½" (6cm) strips	Block B
Fabric 2	¾ yd. (69cm)	• (1) 7½" (19cm) strip	Block A
		• (2) 4½" (11cm) strips	Block B
Fabric 3	¾ yd. (69cm)	• (1) 8" (20cm) strip	Block A
		• (2) 6½" (17cm) strips	Block B
Quilt Back	1¼ yds. (1.1m)	(refer to page 35)	Quilt Back
Binding	½ yd. (46cm)	(refer to page 40)	Quilt Binding

TWIN QUILT (SHOWN)
Finished Blocks: 12" × 12" (30cm × 30cm)
Finished Quilt: 60" × 84" (152cm × 213cm)

FABRIC	YARDAGE	CUTS	FOR
Fabric 1	1¾ yds. (1.6m)	• (4) 5" (13cm) strips	Block A
		• (3) 5½" (14cm) strips	Block A
		• (5) 2½" (6cm) strips	Block B
Fabric 2	1¾ yds. (1.6m)	• (3) 7½" (19cm) strips	Block A
		• (5) 4½" (11cm) strips	Block B
Fabric 3	2¼ yds. (2m)	• (4) 8" (20cm) strips	Block A
		• (5) 6½" (17cm) strips	Block B
Quilt Back	4 yds. (3.7m)	(refer to page 35)	Quilt Back
Binding	¾ yd. (69cm)	(refer to page 40)	Quilt Binding

For metric measurements, refer to the charts on page 79.

CONSTRUCT THE A BLOCK

1 Make the first strip set. Sew an 8" strip of Fabric 3 to a 5" strip of Fabric 1. Press seam allowances toward Fabric 1. Make one strip set for the small quilt or four for the twin quilt.

2 Cut the strip set into sections every 8" (20cm). (This is easily done with a large square ruler, a combination of two rulers or by using the grid on your cutting mat.) This is Unit 1A. Make five 1A units for the small quilt or twenty for the twin quilt.

Fabric 3

Fabric 1

Make Strip Set

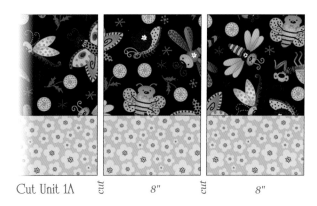

Cut Unit 1A   *cut*   8"   *cut*   8"

3 Make the second strip set. Sew a 5½" strip of Fabric 1 to a 7½" strip of Fabric 2. Press seam allowances toward Fabric 2. Make one strip set for the small quilt or three for the twin quilt.

4 Cut the strip set into sections every 5" (13cm). This is Unit 2A. Make five 2A units for the small quilt or twenty for the twin quilt.

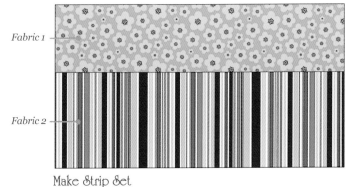

Fabric 1

Fabric 2

Make Strip Set

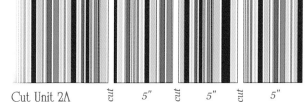

Cut Unit 2A   *cut*   5"   *cut*   5"   *cut*   5"

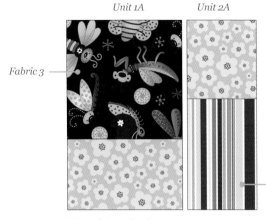

Unit 1A   *Unit 2A*

Fabric 3

Fabric 2

Complete Block A

5 Next to your sewing machine, make a Unit 1A pile, all oriented with Fabric 3 at the top, and a Unit 2A pile, all oriented with Fabric 2 at the bottom. Flip a Unit 2A onto a Unit 1A, right sides together and edges aligned, and chain piece to make the A blocks. Press. Each block should measure 12½" × 12½" (32cm × 32cm). Make five A blocks for the small quilt or twenty for the twin quilt.

3-Fabric Tip

When working with stripes, it is important to know that the stripes are not always printed exactly straight. Whenever I cut stripes with my rotary ruler, I make sure the stripes are aligned with the straight lines in the ruler, so that the stripe will look straight in the quilt.

CONSTRUCT THE B BLOCK

1 Make the next strip set. Sew strips together in this order: a 6½" strip of Fabric 3, a 2½" strip of Fabric 1 and a 4½" strip of Fabric 2. Press all seam allowances in one direction. Make two strip sets for the small quilt or five for the twin quilt.

2 Cut the strip sets into sections every 12½" (32cm). This is Block B. Press. Each block should measure 12½" × 12½" (32cm × 32cm). Make five B blocks for the small quilt or fifteen for the twin quilt.

Fabric 3

Fabric 1

Fabric 2

Make Strip Set

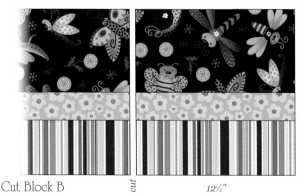

Cut Block B   *cut*   *12½"*

ASSEMBLE AND FINISH THE QUILT

1 Arrange the blocks in a design that you like, either symmetrically or randomly. It may help to lay them out on a bed or on the floor. For the small quilt, you will have an extra block. Use it to make a coordinating pillow!

2 For the small quilt, sew the blocks into **three rows of three blocks**. For the twin quilt, sew the blocks into **seven rows of five blocks**. Press seam allowances of even-numbered rows in one direction; press seam allowances of odd-numbered rows in the opposite direction. Sew the rows together to complete the quilt top.

3 Carefully press and square off the quilt top, and prepare the backing and batting. Layer and pin the quilt, referring to page 36.

4 For functional quilting, stitch-in-the-ditch. Use the template provided on page 122 for more decorative quilting.

5 Bind the quilt to finish.

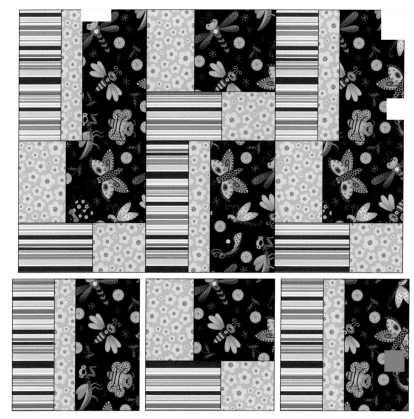

Small Quilt Symmetrical Layout

Block A Template Quilting Pattern

Block B Template Quilting Pattern

82

Twin Quilt Random Layout

Piano Keys

I love the way these two blocks mix and match. Move them together to form larger squares, or twist and turn them for a quilt with lots of visual excitement.

CHOOSING FABRICS:

- Fabric 1: lightest value, large-scale print (floral print in sample)
- Fabric 2: darkest value, medium-scale print (blue in sample)
- Fabric 3: medium value, small-scale print (pink in sample)
- Backing fabric
- Binding fabric: complementary fabric of your choice

84

• *All strips are cut the width of the fabric (WOF),*
approximately 42" to 45" (107cm to 114cm).
• *Fabric used for the quilt back must measure at*
least 43" (109cm) wide.

SMALL QUILT (SHOWN)
Finished Blocks: 7" × 14" (18cm × 36cm)
Finished Quilt: 42" × 42" (107cm × 107cm)

FABRIC	YARDAGE	CUTS	FOR
Fabric 1	1¼ yds. (1.1m)	• (2) 9½" (24cm) strips	Block A
		• (5) 2¼" (6cm) strips	Block B
Fabric 2	¾ yd. (69cm)	• (4) 2¼" (6cm) strips	Block A
		• (5) 2¼" (6cm) strips	Block B
Fabric 3	1 yd. (91cm)	• (4) 2¼" (6cm) strips	Block A
		• (2) 6½" (17cm) strips	Block B
Quilt Back	1¼ yds. (1.1m)	(refer to page 35)	Quilt Back
Binding	½ yd. (46cm)	(refer to page 40)	Quilt Binding

TWIN QUILT
Finished Blocks: 7" × 14" (18cm × 36cm)
Finished Quilt: 63" × 84" (160cm × 213cm)

FABRIC	YARDAGE	CUTS	FOR
Fabric 1	2¾ yds. (2.5m)	• (6) 9½" (24cm) strips	Block A
		• (14) 2¼" (6cm) strips	Block B
Fabric 2	1½ yds. (1.4m)	• (8) 2¼" (6cm) strips	Block A
		• (14) 2¼" (6cm) strips	Block B
Fabric 3	1¾ yds. (1.6m)	• (8) 2¼" (6cm) strips	Block A
		• (6) 6½" (17cm) strips	Block B
Quilt Back	4 yds. (3.7m)	(refer to page 35)	Quilt Back
Binding	¾ yd. (69cm)	(refer to page 40)	Quilt Binding

CONSTRUCT THE A BLOCK

1 Make the strip set. Sew strips together in this order: a 2¼" strip of Fabric 2, a 2¼" strip of Fabric 3, a 2¼" strip of Fabric 2 and a 2¼" strip of Fabric 3. Press seam allowances toward the Fabric 2 edge. Make two strip sets for the small quilt or four for the twin quilt.

2 Cut the strip sets into sections every 5½" (14cm). This is Unit A. Make nine Unit A pieces for the small quilt or twenty-seven for the twin quilt.

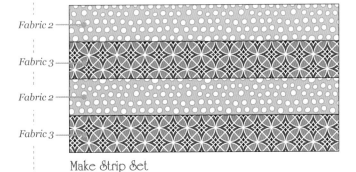

Fabric 2
Fabric 3
Fabric 2
Fabric 3

Make Strip Set

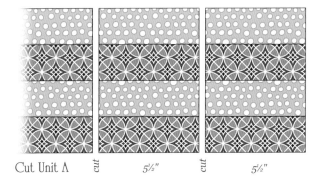

Cut Unit A   *cut*   *5½"*   *cut*   *5½"*

3 Place a 9½" strip of Fabric 1 right-side-up in the sewing machine. Place Unit A right-side-down on the strip so that the Fabric 3 piece is at the top. With the right-hand raw edges aligned, sew the unit to the strip. Sew all the Unit A pieces to the 9½" Fabric 1 strips in this way.

4 Press the seam allowances toward the Fabric 1 strip. Cut the sections apart at the edges of the units. This is now Block A. Press. Each block should measure 7½" × 14½" (19cm × 37cm). Make nine blocks for the small quilt or twenty-seven for the twin quilt.

86

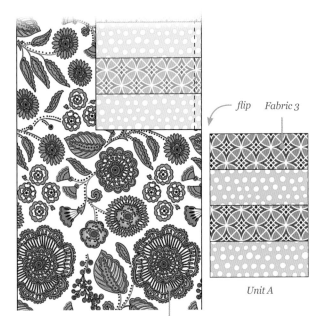

flip   Fabric 3

Sew Units to Strip   *Fabric 1 strip*

Unit A

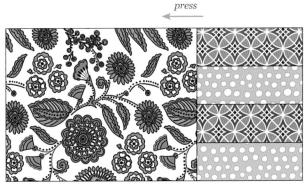

press

Complete Block A

CONSTRUCT THE B BLOCK

1 Make the strip set. Sew strips together in this order: a 2¼" strip of Fabric 2, a 2¼" strip of Fabric 1, a 2¼" strip of Fabric 2 and a 2¼" strip of Fabric 1. Make 2½ strip sets for the small quilt and 7 strip sets for the twin quilt.

Note: To make half a strip set, sew a Fabric 2 strip to a Fabric 3 strip, press, fold in half lengthwise and cut at the fold. Now sew these two pieces together to form the half strip set.

2 Press the seam allowances toward the Fabric 2 edge. Cut the strip sets into sections every 8½" (22cm). (This is easily done with a large square ruler, a combination of two rulers or by using the grid on your cutting mat.) This is Unit B. Make nine B units for the small quilt or twenty-seven for the twin quilt.

Fabric 2
Fabric 1
Fabric 2
Fabric 1

Make Strip Set

Cut Unit B   cut   8½"

3 Place a 6½" strip of Fabric 3 right-side-up in the sewing machine. Place Unit B right-side-down on the strip so that the Fabric 1 piece is at the top. With the right-hand raw edges aligned, sew the unit to the strip. Sew all the Unit A pieces to the 6½" Fabric 3 strips in this way.

4 Press the seam allowances toward the Fabric 3 strip. Cut the sections apart at the edges of the units. This is Block B. Press. Each block should measure 7½" × 14½" (19cm × 37cm). Make nine blocks for the small quilt or twenty-seven for the twin quilt.

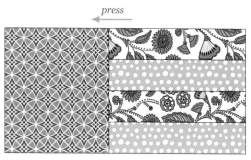

press

Complete Block B

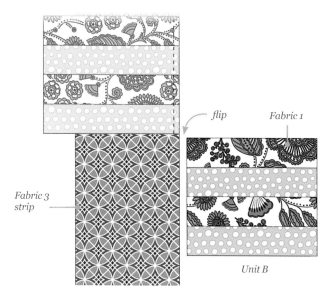

Fabric 3 strip

flip   *Fabric 1*

Unit B

Sew Units to Strip

ASSEMBLE AND FINISH THE QUILT

1 Arrange the blocks in any design that you like, either symmetrically or randomly. It may help to lay them out on a bed or on the floor.

Note: For a symmetrical arrangement, sew three-block units, as shown, and lay them out so that every other unit is rotated horizontally or vertically.

Note: For an asymmetrical arrangement, lay out the design as you like it. In the case of the sample quilt, the blocks are not arranged in row order, but rather in sections.

2 Depending on your chosen layout, sew the blocks into rows, sections, or in any logical order to complete the quilt top.

3 Carefully press and square off the quilt top, and prepare the backing and batting. Layer and pin the quilt, referring to page 36.

4 For functional quilting, stitch-in-the-ditch around each block, between the large squares and the piano keys. Or use the template provided on page 123 for decorative quilting.

5 Bind the quilt to finish.

3-Block Units

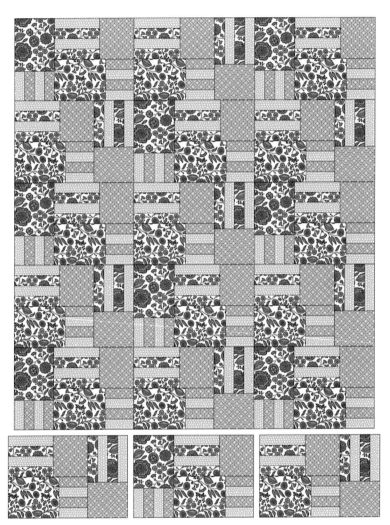

Twin Quilt Symmetrical Layout

Block A Template Quilting Pattern

Block B Template Quilting Pattern

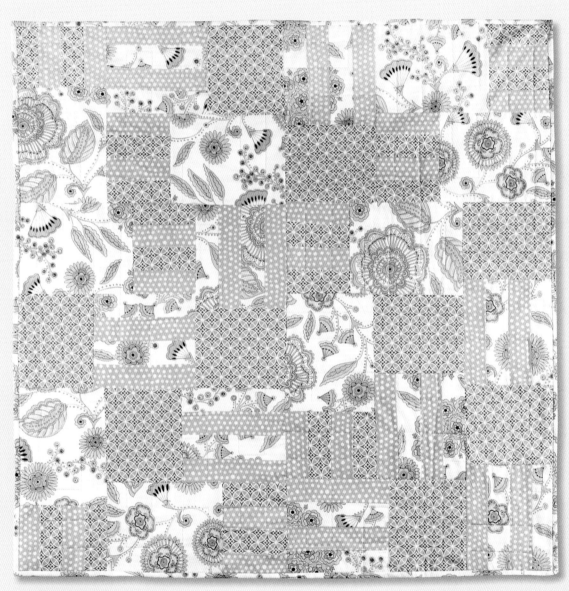

Small Quilt Random Layout

Block and a Half

Who says all quilt blocks have to be the same size?
These two blocks are designed to fit together in a wide
variety of designs—the smaller block is exactly half the
width of the larger block, so mix and match them in
any arrangement you like!

CHOOSING FABRICS:

- Fabric 1: focus fabric, largest-scale print (orange floral
  in sample)

- Fabric 2: darker print (aqua print in sample)

- Fabric 3: lighter print (white/orange print in sample)

- Backing fabric

- Binding fabric: complementary fabric of your choice

• All strips are cut the width of the fabric (WOF), approximately 42" to 45" (107cm to 114cm).

• Fabric used for the quilt back must measure at least 42" (107cm) wide.

• Depending on the true width of your fabric, you may need to cut additional strips. The yardage for any additional strips is built into the yardage requirements below.

SMALL QUILT

Finished Block A: 10" × 10" (25cm × 25cm)
Finished Block B: 10" × 5" (25cm × 13cm)
Finished Quilt: 40" × 40" (102cm × 102cm)

FABRIC	YARDAGE	CUTS	FOR
Fabric 1	1 yd. (91cm)	• (1) 2½" (6cm) strip	Block A, Unit 1
		• (2) 7½" (19cm) strips	Block A, Unit 1
		• (2) 3½" (9cm) strips	Block B
Fabric 2	¾ yd. (69cm)	• (1) 4½" (11cm) strip	Block A, Unit 1
		• (2) 5½" (14cm) strips	Block A, Unit 2
		• (2) 3½" (9cm) strips	Block B
Fabric 3	¾ yd. (69cm)	• (2) 5½" (14cm) strips	Block A, Unit 2
		• (4) 2½" (6cm) strips	Block B
Quilt Back	1¼ yds. (1.1m)	(refer to page 35)	Quilt Back
Binding	½ yd. (46cm)	(refer to page 40)	Quilt Binding

TWIN QUILT (SHOWN)

Finished Block A: 10" × 10" (25cm × 25cm)
Finished Block B: 10" × 5" (25cm × 13cm)
Finished Quilt: 60" × 80" (152cm × 203cm)

FABRIC	YARDAGE	CUTS	FOR
Fabric 1	2¼ yds. (1.1m)	• (3) 2½" (6cm) strips	Block A, Unit 1
		• (6) 7½" (19cm) strips	Block A, Unit 1
		• (5) 3½" (9cm) strips	Block B
Fabric 2	1¾ yds. (1.6m)	• (3) 4½" (11cm) strips	Block A, Unit 1
		• (4) 5½" (14cm) strips	Block A, Unit 2
		• (5) 3½" (9cm) strips	Block B
Fabric 3	1½ yds. (1.4m)	• (4) 5½" (14cm) strips	Block A, Unit 2
		• (10) 2½" (6cm) strips	Block B
Quilt Back	4 yds. (3.7m)	(refer to page 35)	Quilt Back
Binding	¾ yd. (69m)	(refer to page 40)	Quilt Binding

CONSTRUCT THE A BLOCK

1 Make the strip set. Sew a 4½" strip of Fabric 2 to a 2½" strip of Fabric 1. Press seam allowances toward Fabric 1. Make one strip set for the small quilt or three for the twin quilt. Cut the strip set into sections every 3½" (9cm). This is Unit 1A. Make twelve 1A units for the small quilt or thirty-six for the twin quilt.

Fabric 2 —

Fabric 1 —

Make Unit 1A — cut — 3½" — cut — 3½" — cut — 3½"

92

2 Place a 7½" strip of Fabric 1 right-side-up in the sewing machine. Place Unit 1A right-side-down on the strip so that the Fabric 2 piece is at the top. With the right-hand raw edges aligned, sew the unit to the strip. Sew all the Unit 1A pieces to the 7½" Fabric 1 strips in this way.

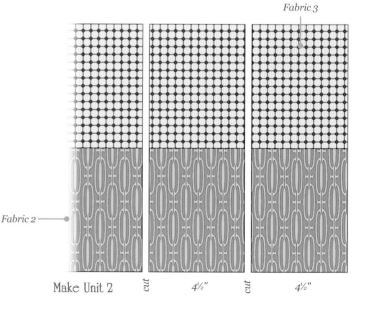

Fabric 1 strip

flip

Fabric 2

Unit 1A

Sew Units to Strip

3 Press the seam allowances toward the Fabric 1 strip. Cut the sections apart at the edges of the units, lining up the seams with your ruler. This is now Unit 1.

press

Complete Unit 1

4 Make the second strip set. Sew a 5½" strip of Fabric 3 to a 5½" strip of Fabric 2. Press the seam allowance toward Fabric 2. Make two strip sets for the small quilt or four for the twin quilt. Cut the strip set into sections every 4½"(11cm). This is Unit 2. Make twelve Unit 2 sections for the small quilt or thirty-six for the twin quilt.

Fabric 3

Fabric 2 —

Make Unit 2 — cut — 4½" — cut — 4½"

Unit 1   Unit 2

Fabric 2

Fabric 3

Complete Block A

5 Next to your sewing machine, make a Unit 1 pile, all oriented with Fabric 2 at the top, and a Unit 2 pile, all oriented with Fabric 3 at the top. Flip a Unit 2 onto a Unit 1, right sides together, and chain piece along the edge to make Block A. Press. Each block should measure 10½" × 10½" (27cm × 27cm). Make twelve A blocks for the small quilt or thirty-four for the twin quilt.

Note: There are more blocks than needed for either quilt to allow for flexibility in the design.

CONSTRUCT THE B BLOCK

1 Make the strip set. Sew strips together in this order: a 3½" strip of Fabric 2, a 2½" strip of Fabric 3, a 3½" strip of Fabric 1 and a 2½" strip of Fabric 3. Press seam allowances in one direction. Make two strip sets for the small quilt or five for the twin quilt.

2 Cut the strip set into sections every 5½". This is Block B. Press. Each block should measure 10½" × 5½" (27cm × 14cm). Make ten B blocks for the small quilt or thirty or more for the twin quilt.

Note: For the small quilt, the yardage will yield more than ten B blocks; these can be used in place of some of the A blocks, if you prefer.

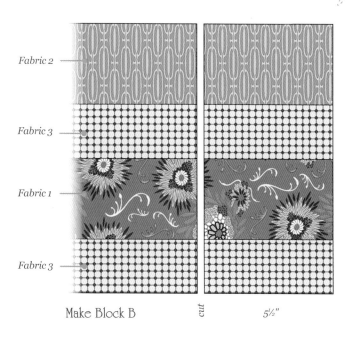

Fabric 2

Fabric 3

Fabric 1

Fabric 3

Make Block B   cut   5½"

ASSEMBLE AND FINISH THE QUILT

1 Arrange the blocks in any design that you like, either symmetrically or randomly. It may help to lay them out on a bed or on the floor. For the small quilt, arrange the blocks into **four rows of four blocks**. For the twin quilt, arrange the blocks into **eight rows of six blocks**.

2 Depending on your arrangement, it may be more logical to sew your quilt together in sections rather than rows. (In the sample quilt, the A Blocks are joined side by side to make a row, and the B Blocks are joined end to end to make a row. These rows are then alternated.) Once you have a design you like, join the blocks into rows or sections, and then join the rows or sections to complete the quilt top.

3 Carefully press and square off the quilt top, and prepare the backing and batting. Layer and pin the quilt, referring to page 36.

4 For functional quilting, stitch-in-the-ditch around each block and at the edges of Fabrics 1 and 2. Or use the template provided on page 123 for decorative quilting.

5 Bind the quilt to finish.

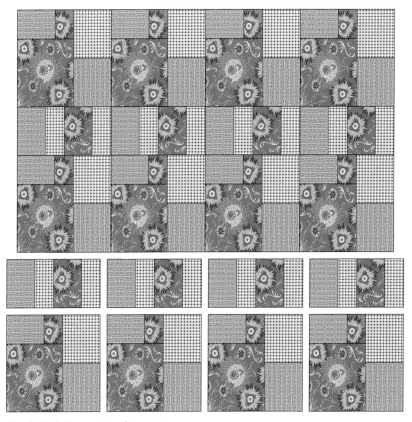

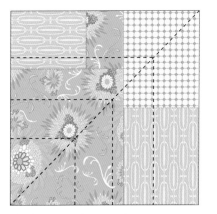

Small Quilt Symmetrical Layout

Block A Template Quilting Pattern

Block B Template
Quilting Pattern

Note: If you prefer not to use a template for Block B, use the seams as the guide for quilting by running the left edge of your quilting foot along the seam—no template required!

Twin Quilt Random Layout

Quick Flip Strips

Do you want a fast and easy project? They don't
get much easier than this! One strip set is cut into
sections and it all goes together in a snap. Use prints
with contrasting colors and a variety of scale.

CHOOSING FABRICS:

- Fabric 1: largest-scale print or focus
  fabric (green print in sample)

- Fabric 2: complement to Fabric 1,
  medium-scale (red/orange print
  in sample)

- Fabric 3: contrast or accent color,
  small-scale (blue in sample)

- Backing fabric

- Binding fabric: complementary fabric
  of your choice

• All strips are cut the width of the fabric (WOF), approximately 42" to 45" (107cm to 114cm).
• Fabric used for the quilt back must measure at least 43" (109cm) wide.

SMALL QUILT (SHOWN)
Finished Quilt: 36" × 36" (91cm × 91cm)

FABRIC	YARDAGE	CUTS	FOR
Fabric 1	1 yd. (91cm)	• (3) 5½" (14cm) strips	Strip Set
		• (3) 3" (8cm) strips	Strip Set
Fabric 2	½ yd. (46cm)	• (3) 4" (10cm) strips	Strip Set
Fabric 3	¼ yd. (23cm)	• (3) 1½" (4cm) strips	Strip Set
Quilt Back	1¼ yds. (1.1m)	(refer to page 35)	Quilt Back
Binding	½ yd. (46cm)	(refer to page 40)	Quilt Binding

TWIN QUILT
Finished Quilt: 60" × 72" (152cm × 183cm)

FABRIC	YARDAGE	CUTS	FOR
Fabric 1	2¾ yds. (2.5m)	• (10) 5½" (14cm) strips	Strip Set
		• (10) 3" (8cm) strips	Strip Set
Fabric 2	1¼ yds. (1.1m)	• (10) 4" (10cm) strips	Strip Set
Fabric 3	½ yd. (46cm)	• (10) 1½" (4cm) strips	Strip Set
Quilt Back	4 yds. (3.7m)	(refer to page 35)	Quilt Back
Binding	¾ yd. (69cm)	(refer to page 40)	Quilt Binding

For metric measurements, refer to the charts on page 97.

CONSTRUCT THE STRIP SET

1 Join strips together in this order: a 3" strip of Fabric 1, a 1½" strip of Fabric 3, a 5½" strip of Fabric 1 and a 4" strip of Fabric 2. Press the seam allowances toward Fabric 2. Make three strip sets for the small quilt or ten for the twin quilt. The strip sets should measure 12½" (32cm) wide.

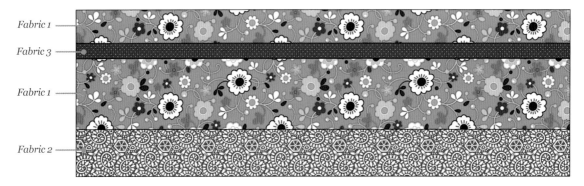

Fabric 1
Fabric 3
Fabric 1
Fabric 2

Make Strip Set

2 Square off both ends of each strip set. From one end of the strip set, cut a 12½" (32cm) square using either a large ruler or the grid on your mat. Set this square aside.

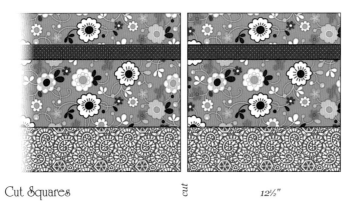

Cut Squares

cut

12½"

3 Carefully fold the remaining strip set in half with right sides together, making sure that the seams line up.

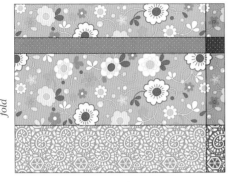

fold

Fold Strip Set in Half, Aligning Seams

4 Align the 12¼" (31cm) line of a large square ruler with the folded edge. Cut along the edge of the square ruler. Open up the fold. This rectangle should measure 24½" × 12½" (62cm × 32cm). Repeat to cut a 12½" (32cm) square and a 24½" (62cm) rectangle from each strip set.

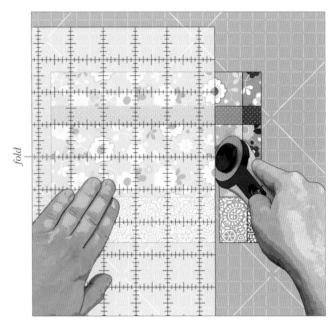

fold

Cut Rectangle

5 Sew one 12½" (32cm) square to the end of each rectangle, flipping the square so the fabrics in the square are opposite the rectangle. Make three sections like this for the small quilt or ten sections for the twin quilt.

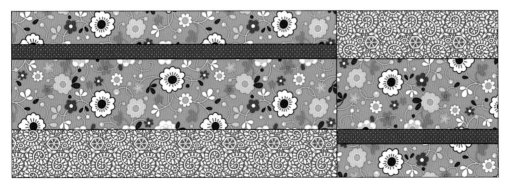

Complete Sections

ASSEMBLE AND FINISH THE QUILT

1 Join the sections together to complete the quilt top.

For the small quilt, join the **three sections** side by side, rotating the center section 180 degrees.

For the twin quilt, arrange the **ten sections** in the order shown at right. Sew the top five sections together to make the top half of the quilt. Sew the bottom five sections together to make the bottom half. Sew the two halves together, carefully lining up the columns.

2 Carefully press and square off the quilt top, and prepare the backing and batting. Layer and pin the quilt, referring to page 36.

3 For functional quilting, stitch-in-the-ditch around the strips and squares. Use the template provided on page 124 for more decorative quilting.

4 Bind the quilt to finish.

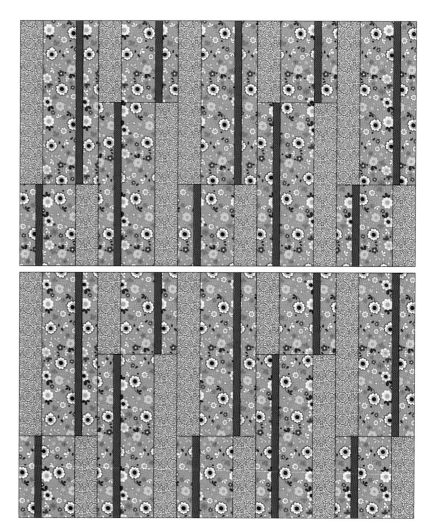

Twin Quilt Layout

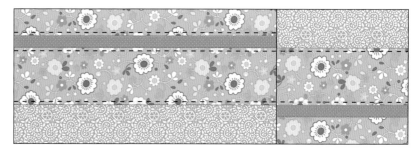

Template Quilting Pattern

Note: If you prefer to not use the template, use the seams as a guide for the edge of the quilting foot.

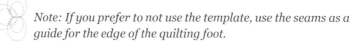

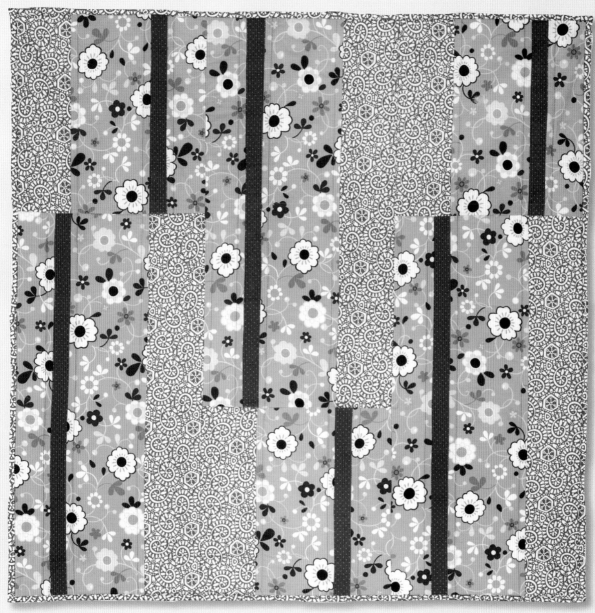

Small Quilt Layout

20 × 20

Using strip sets to make blocks that are 20" × 20" (51cm × 51cm) makes quick work of finishing a quilt top. Just four blocks make a small quilt and only twelve are needed for a twin-size quilt.

CHOOSING FABRICS:

- Fabric 1: lightest value (pink print in sample)

- Fabric 2: medium value (purple/green bird print in sample)

- Fabric 3: darkest value (dark purple in sample)

- Backing fabric

- Binding fabric: complementary fabric of your choice

• All strips are cut the width of the fabric (WOF), approximately 42" to 45" (107cm to 114cm).
• Fabric used for the quilt back must measure at least 42" (107cm) wide.

SMALL QUILT (SHOWN)
Finished Block: 20" × 20" (51cm × 51cm)
Finished Quilt: 40" × 40" (102cm × 102cm)

FABRIC	YARDAGE	CUTS	FOR
Fabric 1	½ yd. (46cm)	• (1) 5½" (14cm) strip	Unit A
		• (1) 3½" (9cm) strip	Unit A
		• (1) 6½" (17cm) strip	Unit B
Fabric 2	¾ yd. (69cm)	• (1) 6½" (17cm) strip	Unit A
		• (1) 6½" (17cm) strip	Unit B
		• (1) 4½" (11cm) strip	Unit B
Fabric 3	¾ yd. (69cm)	• (1) 6½" (17cm) strip	Unit A
		• (2) 2½" (6cm) strips	Unit B
		• (2) 4½" (11cm) strips	Center
Quilt Back	1¼ yds. (1.1cm)	(refer to page 35)	Quilt Back
Binding	½ yd. (46cm)	(refer to page 40)	Quilt Binding

TWIN QUILT
Finished Block: 20" × 20" (51cm × 51cm)
Finished Quilt: 60" × 80" (152cm × 203cm)

FABRIC	YARDAGE	CUTS	FOR
Fabric 1	1½ yds. (1.4m)	• (3) 5½" (14cm) strips	Unit A
		• (3) 3½" (9cm) strips	Unit A
		• (3) 6½" (17cm) strips	Unit B
Fabric 2	1¾ yds. (1.6m)	• (3) 6½" (17cm) strips	Unit A
		• (3) 6½" (17cm) strips	Unit B
		• (3) 4½" (11cm) strips	Unit B
Fabric 3	2 yds. (1.8m)	• (3) 6½" (17cm) strips	Unit A
		• (6) 2½" (6cm) strips	Unit B
		• (6) 4½" (11cm) strips	Center
Quilt Back	4 yds. (3.7m)	(refer to page 35)	Quilt Back
Binding	¾ yd. (69cm)	(refer to page 40)	Quilt Binding

For metric measurements, refer to the charts on page 103.

CONSTRUCT UNIT A

1 Make the first strip set. Sew strips together in this order: a 5½" strip of Fabric 1, a 6½" strip of Fabric 2, a 6½" strip of Fabric 3 and a 3½" strip of Fabric 1. Press seam allowances toward the narrow Fabric 1 strip. Make one strip set for the small quilt or three for the twin quilt.

2 Cut the strip set into sections every 7½" (19cm). (This is easily done with a large square ruler, a combination of two rulers or by using the grid on your cutting mat.) This is Unit A. Make four A units for the small quilt or twelve for the twin quilt.

Fabric 1
Fabric 2
Fabric 3
Fabric 1

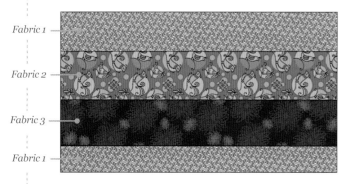

Make Strip Set

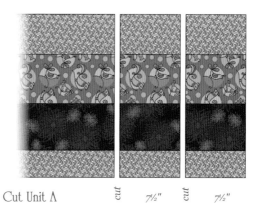

Cut Unit A   *cut* 7½" *cut* 7½"

CONSTRUCT UNIT B

1 Make the second strip set. Sew strips together in this order: a 6½" strip of Fabric 2, a 2½" strip of Fabric 3, a 6½" strip of Fabric 1, a 4½" strip of Fabric 2 and a 2½" strip of Fabric 3. Press seam allowances toward the Fabric 3 strip. Make one strip set for the small quilt or three for the twin quilt.

2 Cut the strip set into sections every 9½" (24cm). This is Unit B. Make four B units for the small quilt or twelve for the twin quilt.

Fabric 2
Fabric 3
Fabric 1
Fabric 2
Fabric 3

Make Strip Set

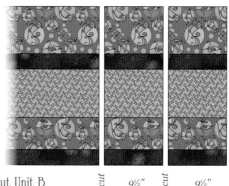

Cut Unit B   *cut* 9½" *cut* 9½"

CONSTRUCT THE BLOCK

1 Blocks are made by sewing the 4½" strip of Fabric 3 between Unit A and Unit B. Cut each of the center strips of Fabric 3 in half by folding the strip selvage to selvage and cutting on the fold.

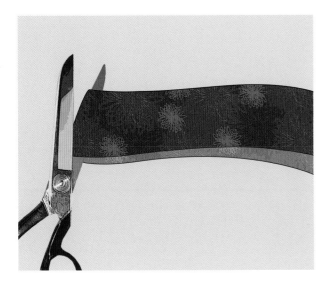

2 Place one Fabric 3 center strip right-side-up in the machine. Place an A unit right sides together with the Fabric 3 strip so that the widest Fabric 1 section is at the top. With the right-hand raw edges aligned, sew the unit to the strip. Sew all of the A units to the Fabric 3 strips in this manner. Press seam allowances toward the center strip.

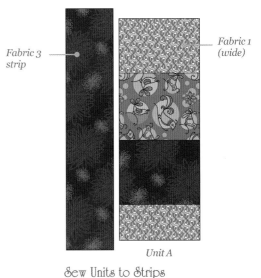

Fabric 3 strip

Fabric 1 (wide)

Unit A

Sew Units to Strips

3 Sew a B unit to the other side of each center strip, being careful to align the B unit with the edges of the A unit. Arrange the B units so that the widest Fabric 2 section is at the top. Press seam allowances toward the center strip. This completes the block. Press and trim the center strip even with the edges of the units. Each block should measure 20½" × 20½" (52cm × 52cm). Make four blocks for the small quilt or twenty blocks for the twin quilt.

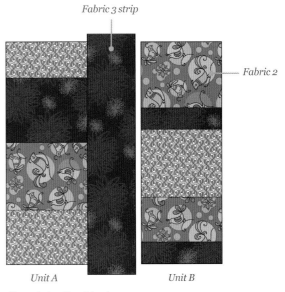

Fabric 3 strip

Fabric 2

Unit A

Unit B

Complete the Block

ASSEMBLE AND
FINISH THE QUILT

1 Rotate the blocks as desired to make a variety of designs. Sew them into **two rows of two blocks** each for the small quilt, or **four rows of three blocks** each for the twin quilt.

2 Carefully press and square off the quilt top, and prepare the backing and batting. Layer and pin the quilt, referring to page 36.

3 For functional quilting, stitch-in-the-ditch around each center strip and block edges. Use the template provided on page 124 for more decorative quilting.

4 Bind the quilt to finish.

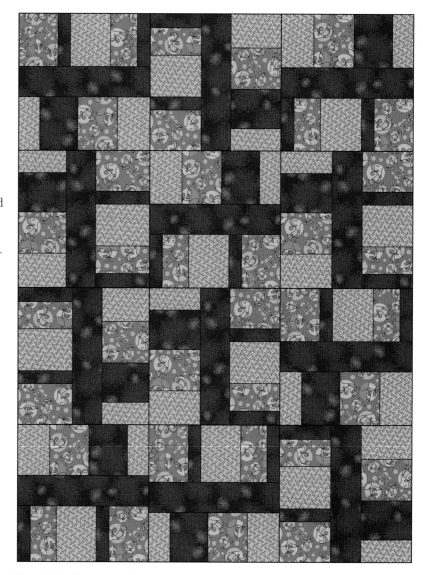

Twin Quilt Symmetrical Layout

Template Quilting Pattern

Small Quilt Random Layout

All in a Row

This quilt is so different from traditional patterns and is much easier to construct than it appears. Using an accent color for the squares will make the design really sing!

108

CHOOSING FABRICS:

- Fabric 1: lightest value, largest-scale print (light blue floral in sample)

- Fabric 2: darkest value (brown in sample)

- Fabric 3: medium value or accent (blue teardrop print in sample)

- Backing fabric

- Binding fabric: complementary fabric of your choice

Note: If using a fabric with a strong directional design (like a stripe), use it as Fabric 3.

• All strips are cut the width of the fabric (WOF), approximately 42" to 45" (107cm to 114cm).
• Fabric used for the quilt back must measure at least 42" (107cm) wide.

SMALL QUILT (SHOWN)
Finished Quilt: 36" × 40" (91cm × 102cm)

FABRIC	YARDAGE	CUTS	FOR
Fabric 1	¾ yd. (69cm)	• (2) 2½" (6cm) strips • (3) 4½" (11cm) strips	Units 1 and 1A Columns
Fabric 2	¾ yd. (69cm)	• (2) 2½" (6cm) strips • (3) 4½" (11cm) strips	Units 1 and 1A Columns
Fabric 3	½ yd. (46cm)	• (2) 4½" (11cm) strips	Unit 2
Quilt Back	1¼ yds. (1.1m)	(refer to page 35)	Quilt Back
Binding	½ yd. (46cm)	(refer to page 40)	Quilt Binding

TWIN QUILT
Finished Quilt: 60" × 80" (152cm × 203cm)

FABRIC	YARDAGE	CUTS	FOR
Fabric 1	2 yds. (1.8m)	• (7) 2½" (6cm) strips • (10) 4½" (11cm) strips	Units 1 and 1A Columns
Fabric 2	2 yds. (1.8m)	• (7) 2½" (6cm) strips • (10) 4½" (11cm) strips	Units 1 and 1A Columns
Fabric 3	1 yd. (91cm)	• (7) 4½" (11cm) strips	Unit 2
Quilt Back	4 yds. (3.7m)	(refer to page 35)	Quilt Back
Binding	¾ yd. (69cm)	(refer to page 40)	Quilt Binding

For metric measurements, refer to the charts on page 109.

CONSTRUCT UNIT 1 AND 1A

1 Sew together one 2½" strip of Fabric 1 and one 2½" strip of Fabric 2. Press seam allowances toward Fabric 2. Make two strip sets for the small quilt or seven for the twin quilt.

2 Cut the strip sets into 4½" (11cm) sections (Unit 1) and 2½" (6cm) sections (Unit 1A). For the small quilt, cut fifteen Unit 1 sections and three Unit 1A sections. For the twin quilt, cut fifty Unit 1 sections and five Unit 1A sections.

Fabric 1

Fabric 2

Make Strip Set

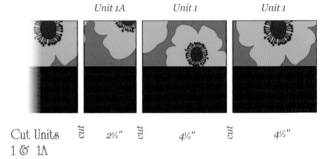

Unit 1A   Unit 1   Unit 1

Cut Units 1 & 1A   cut   2½"   cut   4½"   cut   4½"

110

CONSTRUCT UNIT 2

1 Place one Fabric 3 strip right-side-up in the sewing machine. Place the Unit 1 pieces right-side-down on top of the strip so that the Fabric 2 section is at the top. With the right-hand raw edges aligned, sew the unit to the strip. Sew all the Unit 1 sections to the Fabric 3 strips in this manner. Press seam allowances toward the Fabric 3 strip.

2 Cut the sections apart at the edges of the units. This is now Unit 2. Press seam allowance toward Fabric 3. Make fifteen Unit 2 sections for the small quilt or fifty for the twin quilt. From here, the directions for the small and twin quilts differ slightly.

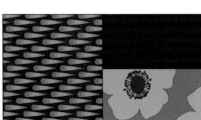

Complete Unit 2

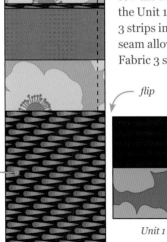

flip

Fabric 3 strip

Fabric 2

Unit 1

Sew Units to Strip

ASSEMBLE THE SMALL QUILT

1 For the small quilt, pin and then stitch Units 1A and 2 end to end in a column in the following order:

Unit 1A
Unit 2
Unit 2
Unit 2
Unit 2
Unit 2

Press seam allowances toward the bottom of the column. Trim the bottom section of the column so that it measures 2¼" (6cm) from the seam edge to the bottom raw edge. Make three columns in this manner for the small quilt.

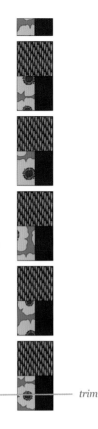

trim

2 Sew each of the columns in between a 4½" strip of Fabric 1 and a 4½" strip of Fabric 2 as shown at right, making sure that corresponding fabrics are next to each other.

3 Press seam allowances toward the outside strips. Trim the ends of the columns even with the center section. Sew the three pieced columns side by side to assemble the small quilt top.

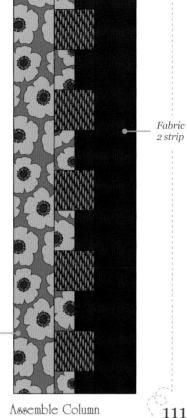

Fabric 2 strip

Fabric 1 strip

Assemble Column

111

ASSEMBLE THE TWIN QUILT

1 To make the columns for the top half of the twin quilt, follow the instructions for Step 1 of *Assemble the Small Quilt*, but do NOT trim the bottom of the columns. Make five columns in this manner.

2 To make the columns for the bottom half of the twin quilt, pin and then stitch five Unit 2 pieces end to end in a column. Press seam allowances toward the bottom of the column. Trim the bottom section of the column so that it measures 2¼" (6cm) from the seam edge to the bottom raw edge (as shown at right). Make five columns in this manner.

top columns   bottom columns

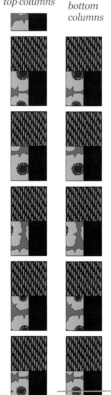

trim (bottom columns only)

3 Sew each of the columns in between a 4½" strip of Fabric 1 and a 4½" strip of Fabric 2 making sure that corresponding fabrics are next to each other (use the illustration above for placement reference). Press seam allowances toward the outside strips. Trim the ends of the outer strips even with the center section.

4 Sew the five top pieced columns side by side and the five bottom pieced columns side by side. Sew the top half of the quilt to the bottom half of the quilt, lining up the columns so that they appear continuous (see page 112 for layout).

FINISH THE QUILT

1 Carefully press and square off the quilt top, and prepare the backing and batting. Layer and pin the quilt, referring to page 36.

2 For functional quilting, stitch-in-the-ditch between all the rows and around each square. Use the template provided on page 125 for more decorative quilting.

Note: To achieve clean corners when quilting, leave the needle in the down position at the corner, lift the presser foot and pivot around the needle. Lower the presser foot and continue.

3 Bind the quilt to finish.

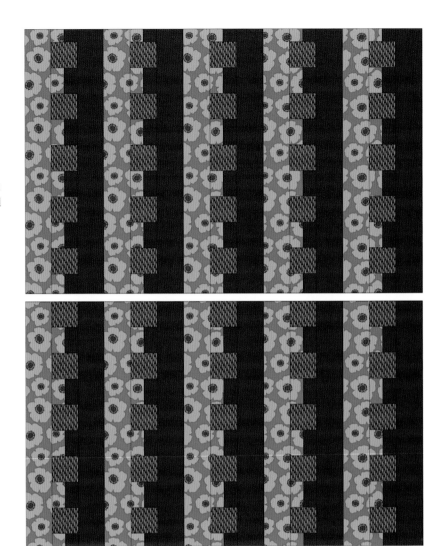

Twin Quilt Layout

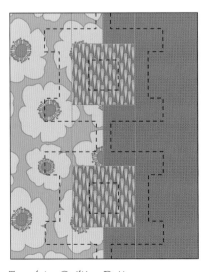

Template Quilting Pattern

Small Quilt Layout

Ode to Op Art

I love the idea of making quilts that look like op art, but most of those I have seen require every corner of every square to be precisely pinned and matched. But not this one! Make a strip set, cut it up and reassemble the strips for a great op art design.

CHOOSING FABRICS:

- Fabric 1: darkest value (black with dots in sample)

- Fabric 2: lightest value (red floral in sample)

- Fabric 3: medium value and/or accent (black and white swirls in sample)

- Backing fabric

- Binding fabric: complementary fabric of your choice

114

Note: Fabrics 1 and 2 should have a strong contrast.

Ode to Op Art

- *All strips are cut the width of the fabric (WOF), approximately 42" to 45" (107cm to 114cm).*
- *Fabric used for the quilt back must measure at least 43" (109cm) wide.*
- *As you cut the strips, keep them in the order listed. Read the Construction steps on page 116 before cutting.*

SMALL QUILT (SHOWN)
Finished Quilt: 41" × 40" (104 × 102)

FABRIC	YARDAGE	CUTS	FOR
Fabric 1	¾ yd. (69cm)	• (1) 6½" (17cm) strip • (1) 2½" (6cm) strip • (1) 3½" (9cm) strip • (1) 3½" (9cm) strip • (1) 5½" (14cm) strip	Strip Set
Fabric 2	¾ yd. (69cm)	• (1) 5½" (14cm) strip • (1) 3½" (9cm) strip • (1) 4½" (11cm) strip • (1) 4½" (11cm) strip • (1) 5½" (17cm) strip	Strip Set
Fabric 3	¼ yd. (23cm)	• (2) 3½" (9cm) strips	Strip Set
Quilt Back	1¼ yds. (1.1m)	(refer to page 35)	Quilt Back
Binding	½ yd. (46cm)	(refer to page 40)	Quilt Binding

TWIN QUILT
Finished Quilt: 63" × 83" (XX × XX)

FABRIC	YARDAGE	CUTS	FOR
Fabric 1	2 yds. (1.8m)	• (3) 6½" (17cm) strips • (3) 2½" (6cm) strips • (3) 3½" (9cm) strips • (3) 3½" (9cm) strips • (3) 5½" (14cm) strips	Strip Set
Fabric 2	2¼ yds. (2m)	• (3) 5½" (14cm) strips • (3) 3½" (9cm) strips • (3) 4½" (11cm) strips • (3) 4½" (11cm) strips • (3) 5½" (14cm) strips	Strip Set
Fabric 3	1 yd. (91cm)	• (8) 3½" (9cm) strip	Strip Set
Quilt Back	4 yds. (3.7m)	(refer to page 35)	Quilt Back
Binding	¾ yd. (69cm)	(refer to page 40)	Quilt Binding

CONSTRUCT THE STRIP SET

1 Start by cutting out the Fabric 1 dark (or "D") strips, laying them out in order from top to bottom as you cut. Leave a space in between between each dark strip as you lay them out.

> **Fabric 1: 6½" D**
> (space)
> **Fabric 1: 2½" D**
> (space)
> **Fabric 1: 3½" D**
> (space)
> **Fabric 1: 3½" D**
> (space)
> **Fabric 1: 5½" D**

2 Cut out the Fabric 2 light (or "L") strips and lay them in the spaces between the dark strips. Sew the strips together in order into a strip set. Make one strip set like this for the small quilt or three for the twin quilt.

> **Fabric 1: 6½" D**
> *Fabric 2: 5½" L*
> **Fabric 1: 2½" D**
> *Fabric 2: 3½" L*
> **Fabric 1: 3½" D**
> *Fabric 2: 4½" L*
> **Fabric 1: 3½" D**
> *Fabric 2: 4½" L*
> **Fabric 1: 5½" D**
> *Fabric 2: 5½" L*

Note: If you get mixed up and confused, don't fret, just keep alternating the light and dark strips. Your quilt won't look exactly like mine, but it will still be great!

3 When all the strips are sewn together, press the seam allowances in one direction. You will have a large piece of striped fabric.

4 Lay this striped fabric flat with the seams running horizontally (as shown). Bring the bottom edge to meet the top edge, with right sides together. Fold in half again, bringing the folded edge to meet the matching edges—just like when folding fabric for rotary cutting. Make sure all the seams are straight and lined up with each other. From here, the directions for the small and twin quilts differ slightly.

For metric measurements, refer to the charts on page 115.

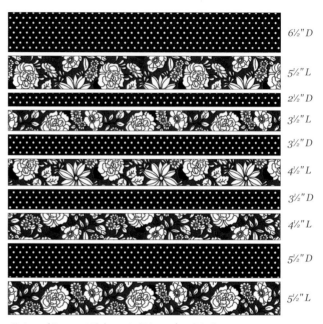

6½" D
5½" L
2½" D
3½" L
3½" D
4½" L
3½" D
4½" L
5½" D
5½" L

Cut and Layout Fabric 1 (D) and 2 (L) Strips

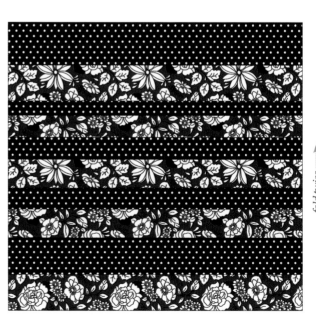

fold twice →

Fold Strip Set in Half, Then Fold in Half Again

116

CONSTRUCT AND FINISH THE SMALL QUILT

1 Using a rotary cutter, make a square-off cut.

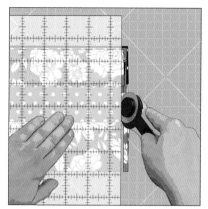

Make Square-Off Cut

2 Cut the following sections from the large strip set: four 8½" (22cm) sections and one 3½" (9cm) section. (This is easily done with a large square ruler, a combination of two rulers or by using the grid on your cutting mat.)

Cut Sections

3 Lay the sections out in the following order, making sure the correct fabric is at the top of each strip:

> 8½" section with Fabric 1 (D) at the top
> 3½" strip of Fabric 3
> 8½" section with Fabric 2 (L) at the top
> 3½" section of Fabric 1 (D) at the top
> 8½" section with Fabric 2 (L) at the top
> 3½" strip of Fabric 3
> 8½" section with Fabric 1 (D) at the top

4 Sew the sections together in order. Press seam allowances toward the 3½" strips. Square off the quilt top, and prepare the backing and batting. Layer and pin the quilt, referring to page 36.

5 For functional quilting, stitch-in-the-ditch along each strip. Or use the template provided on page 125 for decorative quilting.

117

6 Bind the quilt to finish.

Small Quilt Layout

CONSTRUCT AND FINISH THE TWIN QUILT

1 Using a rotary cutter, make a square-off cut, and then cut the following from the three large strip sets: twelve 8½" sections and four 3½" sections.

2 Lay the strips out in the following order, making sure the correct fabric is at the top of each strip:

8½" section with Fabric 1 (D) at the top
3½" strip of Fabric 3
8½" section with Fabric 2 (L) at the top
3½" section with Fabric 1 (D) at the top
8½" section with Fabric 2 (L) at the to
3½" strip of Fabric 3
8½" section with Fabric 1 (D) at the top
3½" section with Fabric 2 (L) at the top
8½" section with Fabric 1 (D) at the top
3½" strip of Fabric 3
8½" section with Fabric 2 (L) at the top

Press seam allowances toward the 3½" strips. Make two identical sections in this way.

3 Sew the two remaining Fabric 3 strips together end-to-end to form one long strip. Sew this strip to the bottom of one strip section. Sew the second strip section to the other side of the Fabric 3 strip to complete the quilt top. Try to line up the sections so that the columns appear to be continuous.

4 Square off the quilt top, and prepare the backing and batting. Layer and pin the quilt, referring to page 36.

5 For functional quilting, stitch-in-the-ditch along each strip. Use the template provided on page 125 for more decorative quilting.

6 Bind the quilt to finish.

118

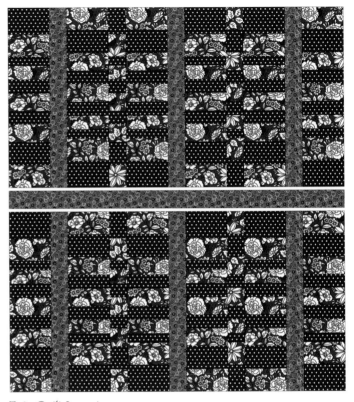

Twin Quilt Layout

Template Quilting Pattern

Small Quilt Layout

Quilting Templates

Enlarge each template at the indicated percentage for accurate results. Use the dotted lines and bold registration marks to line up the quilting template with seams in your quilt. Stitch along the solid lines to quilt your project. Refer to pages 38–39 for more information on using these quilting templates.

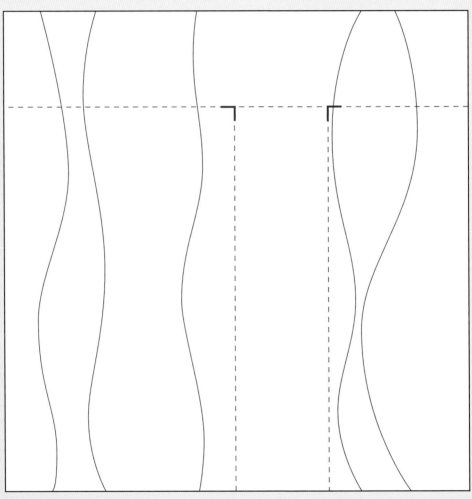

SIMPLICI-T
Reproduce at 200%

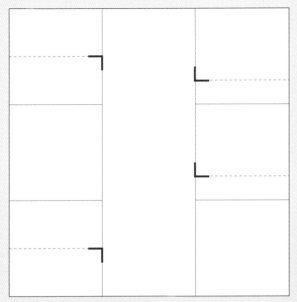

Modern Basket Weave
Reproduce at 400%

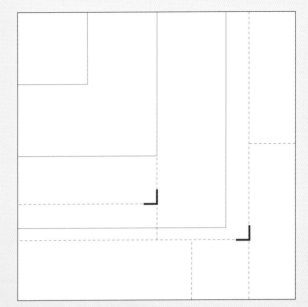

Around the Corner
Reproduce at 400%

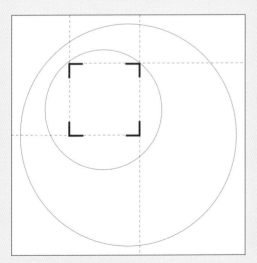

Dancing Squares
Reproduce at 400%

After transferring the enlarged template onto tracing paper, cut out the inner and outer circles. Use the smaller circle template to line up the square and the registration lines on each block, and then position the outer circle around the smaller circle. Pin only the outer circle in place, and then remove the small circle. Quilt along the inside edge for the small circle and the outside edge for the large circle. You should be able to quilt the curves easily with a walking foot. Start stitching each circle on a seam so the starts and stops are less visible. Quilt the smaller circle first so any puckering that occurs moves toward the outside of the block. When stopping to adjust the quilt while sewing the circles, keep the needle in the down position to avoid movement.

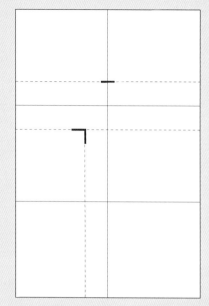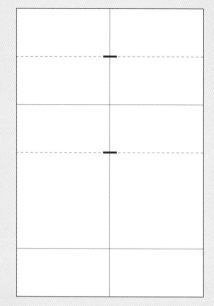

City Windows
Reproduce at 400%

Because the quilting is in straight lines across all the blocks, you can use the template to line up the quilt lines, but use painter's tape (low-tack tape) to mark them. Simply sew along the edge of the tape, pull it up and use it on the next line to be quilted.

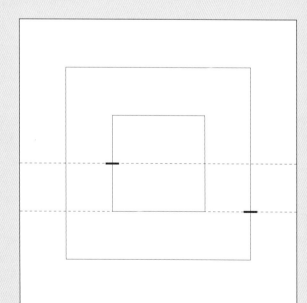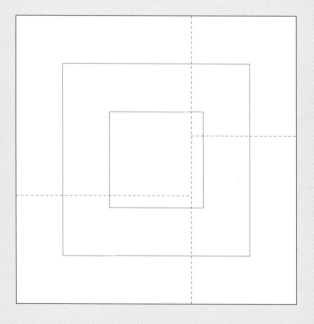

Fun With Stripes
Reproduce at 400%

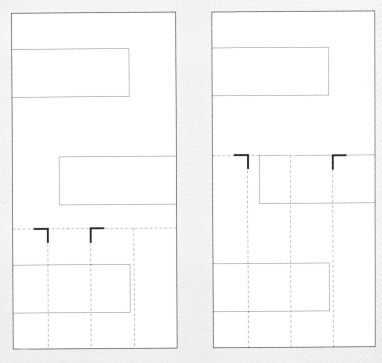

Piano Keys
Reproduce at 400%

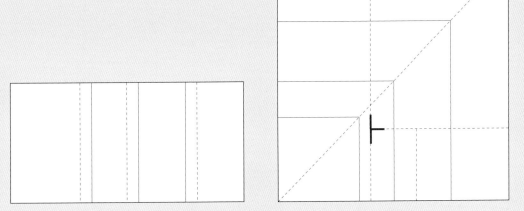

Block and a Half
Reproduce at 400%

Guide the edge of the quilting foot along the block's seams to quilt the smaller block.

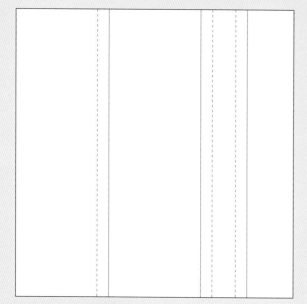

Quick Flip Strip

Reproduce at 400%
Guide the edge of the
quilting foot along the
block's seams to quilt
this block.

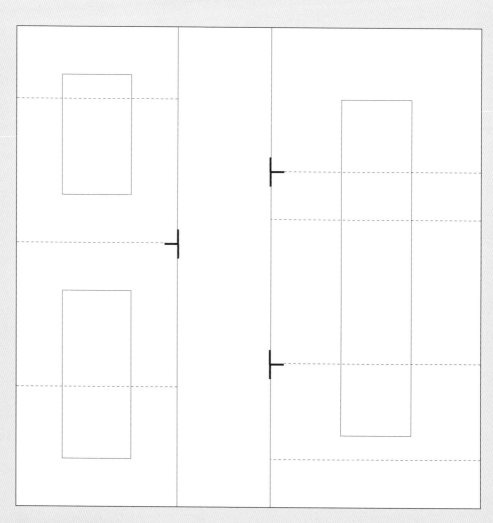

20 x 20 Quilt
Reproduce at 400%

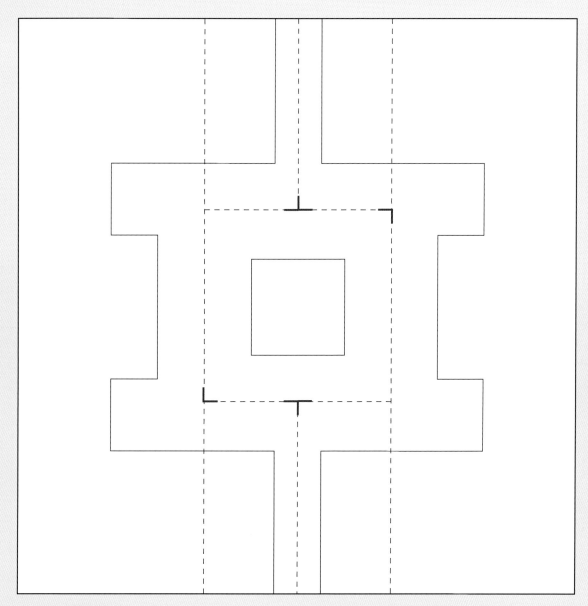

All in a Row
Reproduce at 200%

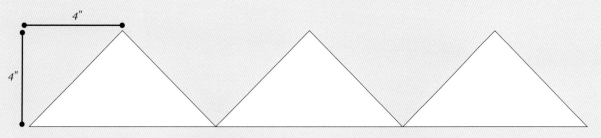

Ode to Op Art
Reproduce at 400%

Align the straight edge along a column seam and stitch along the triangles. Reposition as necessary to quilt the entire length of the quilt, and repeat as desired until the full width of the quilt is secured.

Resources

FABRICS

Amy Butler
www.amybutlerdesign.com

Art Gallery
www.artgalleryquilts.com

FreeSpirit
www.freespiritfabric.com

Michael Miller
www.michaelmillerfabrics.com

Moda
www.unitednotions.com

P&B
www.pbtex.com

RJR
www.rjrfabrics.com

Robert Kaufman
www.robertkaufman.com

Studio E
www.studioefabrics.com
(including the fabrics shown on the cover)

Westminster
www.westminsterfabrics.com

BATTINGS

Fairfield
www.poly-fil.com
(poly and bamboo batting)

Warm and Natural
www.warmcompany.com
(cotton batting)

NOTIONS

Golden Threads Paper
www.goldenthreads.com

Omnigrid Rulers (Prym)
www.dritz.com/brands/omnigrid

Paula Jean Creations
www.paulajeancreations.com
(Kwik Klip tool)

Index

❖ Keep Stitching With These Great Titles! ❖

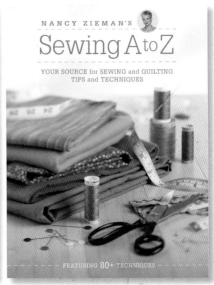

MIXED AND STITCHED
FABRIC INSPIRATION AND HOW-TO'S FOR THE MIXED-MEDIA ARTIST
Jen Osborn

Whether you're a mixed-media artist or a passionate sewer, discover innovative ways to combine fabrics, textures, found objects and more to create meaningful pieces of fabric art. Inside, you'll find step-by-step instructions for sixteen personal projects, "sketchy" stitching techniques, methods for dyeing your own fabric to achieve custom colors for any project and much more!

paperback; 8.25" × 10.875"; 128 pages; Z8073

STRING QUILT REVIVAL
A FRESH APPROACH FOR 13 CLASSIC DESIGNS
Virginia Baker and Barbara Sanders

String quilts have been around for centuries, but in *String Quilt Revival* this time-tested artform is given new life. Virginia Baker and Barbara Sanders guide you through the construction and sewing process of string quilt blocks using no-show mesh stabilizer as a foundation. You will sew thirteen unique string projects, ranging from potholders to queen-size quilts, each featuring a different string block. This book also includes tips and tricks from renowned sewing expert Nancy Zieman.

paperback + DVD; 8.25" × 10.875"; 128 pages; Z9315

NANCY ZIEMAN'S SEWING A TO Z
YOUR SOURCE FOR SEWING AND QUILTING TIPS AND TECHNIQUES
Nancy Zieman

Whether you're a novice sewer or a skilled seamstress, who better to go to for sewing answers and advice than expert Nancy Zieman? Set aside your sewing fears and let Nancy guide you step-by-step through 100+ basic to advanced sewing methods and techniques. Clear instructions and detailed illustrations will help you achieve beautiful results with every project. Stitch with ease with *Nancy Zieman's Sewing A to Z* by your side!

hardcover with concealed wire; 8.25" × 10.875"; 144 pages; Y0005

128